# *A New Approach to Deconstruct and Destroy the ACT*

## *Conquer the ACT with Curvebreakers*

A New Approach to Deconstruct and Destroy the ACT.

Copyright 2020 Curvebreakers Test Prep

curvebreakerstestprep.com

ISBN: 978-0-578-67495-7

# Table of Content

ABOUT THE TEAM/ACKNOWLEDGEMENTS

I would like to thank every Curvebreakers staff member (past and present) for being a part of this journey. Brittany Verlezza, who has been working as a tutor and developing curriculum with Curvebreakers for several years, served as the primary creator and author. While working with students will always be her favorite part of the gig, she was incredibly excited to help create a book that was truly unique by pulling from years of shared experience between us and the rest of the Curvebreakers team. A special thanks to our incredible staff – Michael, Nikki, Michele, Mary, Emily, and more – for their input and contributions.

# FOREWORD FROM THE OWNER OF CURVEBREAKERS, NICK LAPOMA

For the last 14 years standardized tests have been my life. When your sole goal is to teach tests, you must strive to understand them to their core. To truly understand tests is to truly understand their format, scaling, and scoring systems. As you may know, standardized tests are graded on a "curve." This is a statistical concept relating to a bell curve, which is a visualization that shows that a large majority of students will fall within the "bell" of the curve with very few outliers. Those outliers are the highest scorers.

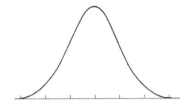

This book shows you how to be an outlier. To do so you do not need to be perfect; you simply need to beat everyone else.

Therein lies the concept of our company "Curvebreakers." We strive to help students break the curve and achieve a higher score. When we started writing this book, our concept was simple: provide you with real, proven strategies that you can implement today. We decided to include no fluff whatsoever. We only included strategies, tips, and tricks that lead to improvement.

That said we are accessible. Feel free to contact us at Info@curvebreakerstestprep.com or call us at (516) 728-1561.

We hope to help you further your educational goals. Now, onto what you came for!


Nick LaPoma


@NickTheTutor on Instagram, Youtube, and Tiktok

Want more? Curvebreakers offers private tutoring for both standardized tests and subject matter, class instruction, and diagnostic practice tests.

## DIANOSTIC PRACTICE EXAMS

Taking practice exams is an important part of studying for a standardized exam. Curvebreakers' unique diagnostic score analysis provides insight into test performance by content, question type, and timing. Students with tutoring packages are able to take an *unlimited amount of diagnostic practice exams at no extra charge.*

curvebreakerstestprep.com/practice-exam-dates/

## PRIVATE TUTORING

Test Prep: Packages include ACT, SAT, PSAT, SSAT, SHSAT, AP Exams, Regents Exams, ISEE, and CHSEE. If you don't see your exam, please inquire with us. Learn more:

curvebreakerstestprep.com/test-prep

Subject Matter Help: For students who need help throughout the school year or summer to review subject content, Curvebreakers offers separate packages for 3rd–8th graders and 9th–12th graders.

curvebreakerstestprep.com/subject-tutoring

## CLASSES & EVENTS

Curvebreakers offers classes and one-time events all year round to prepare students for the SAT, ACT, AP Exams, and Regents Exams. Check out our current schedule online:

curvebreakerstestprep.com/eventsexams/

# HOW TO USE THIS BOOK

There are two major components to test prep: **practicing problems and understanding the exam**. This book is designed to help with the latter. Much of the discussion will be centered around strategies, tangible things that you can do to sharpen your overall test-taking skills and boost your performance. Many of these skills will apply to all standardized tests, not just the ACT, but **the immediate goal is to build fluency in the language of this particular exam.**

While every ACT is different, the test is **repetitive in nature**. This book will provide an intricate breakdown of the exam so that you can recognize these patterns. Before you fight an opponent, you study it, you learn its habits, and you recognize its go-to moves. In doing that, you can predict what's coming and deliver an effective countermove. That's the goal here.

We will discuss the **format** of each section, what **content** you can expect to see, and provide insights to the most **common questions**. That will include different approaches to the questions, information about trick answers (how to spot them and how to avoid them), and some general do's and don'ts to fall back on for each question type.

We will also address foundational skills for each section. That will include effectively reading and annotating, essential math skills, graph-reading basics, properly utilizing the calculator, and the rules for grammar and punctuation. Use those sections to **assess what skills you may need to work on before or during your preparation for the ACT.**

**What you won't find are full practice exams or a large sum of practice questions.** There are some sample questions that are designed to familiarize you with the common questions and answer choices. There are also some sample passages to practice essential reading skills, but we find that it's best to leave the business of creating full practice tests and passages to the makers of the ACT!

<u>**For that reason, this book is meant to be used in conjunction with real exams and diagnostic reports.**</u> Practice, after all, is one of the two core components in test prep, so be sure to work through authentic ACT exams as you read this book. This book can be used at any time – before, during, or after taking the ACT. That being said, your best chance of mastering the exam is by understanding the test **before** you take it.

# WHAT IS A GOOD SCORE?

A good score will vary from student to student and depends mostly on the colleges to which you'll be applying. To determine what score you should aim for, first take a diagnostic test and determine your starting score. Next, compare that score to the scores listed by various college admissions offices and decide which ones seem within reach. This target score should be a few points higher than your score on a diagnostic exam, as you can expect your final score to improve after having spent a few months practicing.

You can use the table below as a reference for where you'd rank compared to the rest of test takers at any given score. The table lists the "percentile rank" for each score, which just means the percentage of test takers who scored less than a given score. For example, the "percentile rank" of a 30 on the English section is 90, which means 90% of test takers scored below a 30.

| Score | English | Math | Reading | Science | Composite |
|-------|---------|------|---------|---------|-----------|
| 36 | 100 | 100 | 100 | 100 | 100 |
| 35 | 99 | 99 | 99 | 99 | 99 |
| 34 | 96 | 99 | 97 | 98 | 99 |
| 33 | 94 | 98 | 95 | 97 | 98 |
| 32 | 93 | 97 | 92 | 96 | 97 |
| 31 | 91 | 96 | 90 | 95 | 95 |
| 30 | 90 | 95 | 87 | 94 | 93 |
| 29 | 88 | 93 | 84 | 92 | 91 |
| 28 | 86 | 91 | 82 | 90 | 88 |
| 27 | 84 | 88 | 80 | 88 | 85 |
| 26 | 82 | 83 | 77 | 85 | 82 |
| 25 | 79 | 79 | 74 | 82 | 78 |
| 24 | 75 | 74 | 71 | 77 | 74 |
| 23 | 70 | 69 | 66 | 70 | 69 |
| 22 | 65 | 65 | 61 | 64 | 64 |
| 21 | 59 | 60 | 54 | 57 | 58 |
| 20 | 54 | 57 | 49 | 50 | 52 |
| 19 | 48 | 53 | 43 | 43 | 46 |
| 18 | 44 | 47 | 38 | 37 | 40 |
| 17 | 40 | 40 | 32 | 30 | 33 |
| 16 | 36 | 31 | 27 | 24 | 27 |
| 15 | 30 | 19 | 22 | 18 | 20 |
| 14 | 23 | 10 | 18 | 13 | 14 |
| 13 | 18 | 3 | 13 | 9 | 9 |
| 12 | 14 | 1 | 9 | 6 | 4 |

| Score | English | Math | Reading | Science | Composite |
|-------|---------|------|---------|---------|-----------|
| 11 | 11 | 1 | 5 | 4 | 1 |
| 10 | 6 | 1 | 2 | 2 | 1 |
| 9 | 3 | 1 | 1 | 1 | 1 |
| 8 | 1 | 1 | 1 | 1 | 1 |
| 7 | 1 | 1 | 1 | 1 | 1 |
| 6 | 1 | 1 | 1 | 1 | 1 |

# FREQUENTLY ASKED QUESTIONS

**Q:** How can I take a practice test?

**A:** Email us at info@curebreakerstestprep.com and we can email you the materials to take a practice test. We also offer **diagnostic grading** services so you can see **exactly what you need to do to improve your score**.

**Q:** How often should I take a practice test, and how much time should I spend preparing for a real test ?

**A:** We suggest that students take a practice test **at least once every 3 weeks** before taking the real SAT or ACT. We suggest this considering that our students will usually have **4 to 6 months to prepare for the exam**. That would allow the student to take **5+ practice tests before taking the real test.** Real tests can be found on ACT.org

**Q:** What is a "real" ACT test?

**A:** A real ACT test is an exam made by the same people that make the ACT you are taking or a test from a prior administration of the exam that they make available online.

**Q:** How is the exam graded?

**A:** There are four sections on the exam – English, Math, Reading, and Science – which will each earn you a score **between 1 and 36**. The score is calculated by converting a raw score (the number of questions you answered correctly) into a scaled score. The scale on each exam will differ. Your **composite score** is the **average** of the individual section scores. The ACT will round scores. If, for example, your composite score is a 27.5, you will earn a 28.

**Q:** What is superscoring?

**A:** Superscoring allows you to **compile one "superscore" using your best section scores from several test administrations.**
    Ex:    **Test 1:** 30 English, 26 Math, 31 Reading, 24 Science, 28 Total
                **Test 2:** 27 English, 28 Math, 28 Reading, 26 Science , 27 Total
                **Superscore:** 30 English, 28 Math, 31 Reading, 26 Science, 29 Total
Not all colleges accept superscoring. **Check with individual colleges to see their respective policies.** This information can usually be found on their website.

**Q:** How many times should I take an official ACT?

**A:** That will depend on a few different factors, but most students will typically sit for 2–3 official exams. Some students will require more exams to hit their goals, and that's perfectly acceptable. A common misconception is that colleges frown upon students taking the exam several times. It is only a red flag if the results are wildly inconsistent, which can send a message that the student did not take the exam seriously.


**Q:** When should I take my first official exam?

**A:** You'll want to give yourself a few months to prepare before you take your first exam. You should complete **at least 15-20 hours of studying** and take **several practice exams** before your first official test.

# THE PSYCHOLOGY OF TESTING: HOW TO PERFORM WELL ON TEST DAY

One of the more overlooked parts of studying for the ACT is the mental preparation required to succeed. All too often students pile intense pressure on themselves, resulting in low test scores when the real exam rolls around. Outside factors such as family, friends, and the looming college acceptance cycle all heavily weigh on the minds of students. That said, students can avoid outside stressors and gain mental fortitude with the right approach.

First, you cannot put too much pressure on yourself. As stated before, a "good" score is relative to where you start and where your goals lie. Instead of trying to jump directly to your goal score, you should try to move your score up in two point stepping stones. This way, you have less chance of severe disappointment.

Second, you need to take the opinions of family and friends with a grain of salt. **You** are the one who needs to take the test, not them. Of course we love our parents and we understand that they simply want us to succeed, but it is very important to find our own motivation to take these tests. The students that want a better score for themselves typically get greater score increases because their motivation is more genuine. If you are simply studying for the ACT to make your parents happy, it will be difficult to stay motivated.

During the test, it is extremely important to move past mistakes and slip-ups. Great test takers do not dwell on the past but simply move on to the next problem just as they did the last. Most of us will be getting many questions wrong on these tests, so it is important to have the right mental approach. Don't let a bad passage or question get you down. Move past it confidently and remember that every new question is a new opportunity.

**If you can reduce outside stressors, become self-motivated, and move past mistakes quickly, you will have a much greater chance of success on test day.**

# TRACK YOUR PROGRESS

If you haven't already, you should **begin by taking a timed, full-length diagnostic exam.** Those results will help you set some short-term and long-term goals.

Again, you should take full-length practice tests every few weeks (although you may find that more frequent exams will benefit you) and record your results here. Be sure to focus on the individual section scores as well the overall score so that you can assess which sections are improving and which ones still need the most work.

## STARTING SCORE

| Date Taken | Exam Name | English Score | Math Score | Reading Score | Science Score | Composite Score |
|---|---|---|---|---|---|---|
| | | | | | | |

*Remember, your composite score is the average of the four section scores. This score is rounded.

## PRACTICE TESTS

| Date Taken | Exam Name | English Score | Math Score | Reading Score | Science Score | Composite Score |
|---|---|---|---|---|---|---|
| | | | | | | |
| | | | | | | |
| | | | | | | |
| | | | | | | |
| | | | | | | |

## OFFICIAL TESTS

| Date Taken | Exam Name | English Score | Math Score | Reading Score | Science Score | Composite Score |
|---|---|---|---|---|---|---|
|  |  |  |  |  |  |  |
|  |  |  |  |  |  |  |
|  |  |  |  |  |  |  |
|  |  |  |  |  |  |  |

Setting reasonable, **incremental** goals is important.

Big changes to your overall score will not happen overnight; it will take time before you see consistent improvements to each of the four sections in a way that will boost the composite score. This is not meant to spook you! Before you begin the test prep process, it's important for you to recognize that your improvement may not always be linear. Composite scores may stay the same or even dip down a bit from time to time, but that is normal! The exam is made up of four sections, so increases in one section (although great!) may not impact your total score in the way you might hope.

That said, with the correct approach, a strong game plan, the right mindset, and sheer determination, we have seen students substantially raise their score. Typically the largest score increases come from students who dedicate six months to a year studying and also have the guidance of an expert. If you follow the guidance of this book, you will improve your score. For more advice on how to improve, visit our website.

# ASSIGNMENTS

Whether you're working with a tutor or working independently, you should **carve out time each week for ACT prep.** Multiple times a week is even better to keep you continuously immersed in the language of the exam! You can keep track of your assignments here.

DATE _____     ASSIGNMENT _____

_____

DATE _____     ASSIGNMENT _____

_____

DATE _____     ASSIGNMENT _____

_____

DATE _____     ASSIGNMENT _____

_____

DATE _____     ASSIGNMENT _____

_____

DATE _____     ASSIGNMENT _____

_____

DATE _____     ASSIGNMENT _____

_____

DATE _____     ASSIGNMENT _____

_____

DATE _____     ASSIGNMENT _____

_____

DATE _____     ASSIGNMENT _____

_____

DATE _____     ASSIGNMENT _____

_____

DATE                    ASSIGNMENT          _____
                                            _____

DATE                    ASSIGNMENT          _____
                                            _____

DATE                    ASSIGNMENT          _____
                                            _____

DATE                    ASSIGNMENT          _____
                                            _____

DATE                    ASSIGNMENT          _____
                                            _____

DATE                    ASSIGNMENT          _____
                                            _____

DATE                    ASSIGNMENT          _____
                                            _____

DATE                    ASSIGNMENT          _____
                                            _____

DATE                    ASSIGNMENT          _____
                                            _____

DATE                    ASSIGNMENT          _____
                                            _____

DATE                    ASSIGNMENT          _____
                                            _____

DATE                    ASSIGNMENT          _____
                                            _____

curvebreakerstestprep.com

DATE                    ASSIGNMENT      _____

_____                         _____

DATE                    ASSIGNMENT      _____

_____                         _____

DATE                    ASSIGNMENT      _____

_____                         _____

DATE                    ASSIGNMENT      _____

_____                         _____

DATE                    ASSIGNMENT      _____

_____                         _____

DATE                    ASSIGNMENT      _____

_____                         _____

DATE                    ASSIGNMENT      _____

_____                         _____

DATE                    ASSIGNMENT      _____

_____                         _____

DATE                    ASSIGNMENT      _____

_____                         _____

# GENERAL TEST-TAKING STRATEGIES

One often overlooked but important aspect of prepping for the ACT is **general standardized test strategy**. Most students want to dive right in to the questions but will overlook basic principles that can substantially impact their score. We will go over those here:

- Time management

  - It is essential that you not only know the exact number of minutes you have per passage or question on the ACT, but that you practice under those time constraints. Proper time management will not always mean working faster, but **working smarter** by **skipping difficult questions and prioritizing certain passages/questions**. Develop a plan for how you will split your time on test day and be sure that you keep an eye on the clock.

- Prioritize

  - All of the questions are worth the same number of raw score points, so it is in your best interest to **complete the easy questions first** or **pick and choose which questions you can complete when time is running out.** "Easy," of course, is a relative term. What you might find simple, someone else may find challenging. **Figure out your own unique strengths and weaknesses** so that you can spend your time wisely on the questions likely to award you points.

- Answer every question

  - There is no penalty for wrong answer choices so you should **put down an answer for every single question** on the exam regardless of time.

- Process of elimination

  - Sometimes, a question will have several answer choices that are **absurd** or can be **disproven** by various means (we will discuss this in greater detail later). You should **strike out those answers** on the page and take them out of consideration. This will greatly **improve your chances when randomly guessing.**

- Knowing what's wrong is just as important as knowing what's right

  - As discussed in the last point, eliminating all of the wrong answer choices in a problem is just as valid as selecting the correct answer. The ACT loves to include answer choices that are *mostly* correct in hopes that you will ignore the problematic parts (harshly worded, not relevant to the question, partly incorrect, etc.) Being able to **pinpoint these issues as grounds for elimination** is crucial. You may find that eliminating the three bad answer choices is how you arrive at the correct answer for a fair amount of the questions.

- Remember that there is only one correct answer to every question

    - The ACT is a standardized test, which means there's no room for debate or subjectivity. **There are rules (both written AND unwritten) that you will need to learn and follow.** This should keep you from internally debating certain answer choices based on *preference*. For example, the ACT will always favor concise and non-redundant answers in the English section, so if you start to say to yourself that *YOU* would write with more words or repeat certain words for emphasis, you're likely going in the wrong direction.

- Read every answer choice

    - You should read each of the answer choices, even if you think you've found the correct one. You may find something better! It may seem like a waste of time, but you should **consider all of your options**. The exam will often include answer choices that are *mostly* correct as distractor answers. You may not recognize the flaws in those choices until you are presented with a better one. Take those few extra seconds to ensure that you have picked the **best possible answer**.

- Use your pencil actively

    - You will hear this piece of advice a lot throughout this book. The ACT is designed to test your ability **to filter out important information quickly and precisely.** You don't get to highlight, color code, or use any of the other visual tools that help our eyes distinguish what's important. All you have is your pencil. Use it wisely to boost your attention to detail! Reading comprehension and detail-orientedness is built into every section of the exam (not just the reading section), so it's crucial that you give yourself as many visual cues as possible to ensure you are reading the questions, answers, and passages carefully.

- Abide by a 5-second rule (or something close to it)

    - We will talk a lot about the importance of time management throughout this book. You cannot allow yourself to linger on questions that are not going your way. You will need to **skip them and return only if time remains.** That can be a difficult habit to stick to, so you can follow a "5-second rule." That doesn't mean you should be able to finish a problem in 5 seconds! If after 5 seconds, or at any time during the solving of a question, you have no idea what to do – you can't think of a formula/ procedure, you can't identify what the underlying topic is, you can't spot any clues in the wording of the question or answer choices, you can't figure out where to locate the information, etc. – you should skip it and look to return in the event that time allows.

## STUDY TIPS

- Mark up your assignments ( **not just wrong answers, but guesses** )

  - Many students make the mistake of "guessing" on a problem, getting it correct, and simply moving on. Those questions must be **analyzed** and **discussed** so you can understand *why* that particular solution or answer is correct. This will ensure that you can answer similar questions correctly on a consistent basis.

- Categorize/label questions by topic

  - Categorization is one of the most important skills for a standardized test. For example, when faced with a grammar question where all of the answer choices are uses (or misuses) of colons and semicolons, you could categorize that question as a punctuation question within the subsection of colons and semicolons. This type of labeling will help you become **fluent in the language of the exam**. Once you know the topic with which you are dealing, you will know exactly how to tackle the problem and **what trap answers to identify and avoid.**

- Time yourself

  - As previously stated, you should **time yourself** not only on full exams, but on partial assignments such as reading passages or science passages. This will help you get used to completing the work within the exam's time constraints.

- Set aside time every week to work on ACT prep

  - **Consistently chipping away at ACT material is the best way to prepare.** As we stated earlier, students that prepare for 6 months or more by studying, taking practice tests, and reading supplementary materials will perform better than students who cram their prep into one or two months. If you **set aside "ACT study time" in your schedule**, you will be more focused on the ACT and have the organizational skills to get the work done.

# ACT ENGLISH

................................................................................................

## WHAT'S THE GIST?

The English section is the first portion of the exam. It is also the longest in terms of question count. You will have **45 minutes** to complete **75 questions**. This section is split into five passages, each containing 15 questions.

Each question is a multiple choice question with four possible answer choices. Not every problem will appear with a physical question; you might simply be provided with four possible corrections to an underlined portion of the text. Many questions will contain a "NO CHANGE" option, which allows you to keep the language in the original text unchanged.

## WHAT CAN YOU EXPECT TO SEE?

The questions on the exam will fall under two major categories: usage and mechanics and rhetorical writing skills. The first tests your ability to follow the rules of Standard English. The second tests your ability to edit writing so that it is clear, purposeful, and organized.

**USAGE AND MECHANICS:** (roughly 40 questions)

Conventions of Standard English:

- Punctuation (commas, colons, semicolons, possessive apostrophes, dashes, and parentheses)
- Sentence structure (parallelism, proper modifiers, identifying/fixing run-ons, fragments, comma splices, and weak conjunctions, etc.)
- Proper verb tense and subject/verb agreement
- Pronoun agreement

**RHETORICAL WRITING SKILLS:** (roughly 35 questions)

Knowledge of Language:

- Deleting redundant and wordy language
- Choosing language consistent with style and tone
- Revising unclear writing
- Word choice and idioms

Organization, Unity, and Cohesion:

- Selecting proper transition words/phrases
- Rearranging sentences/paragraphs
- Selecting effective opening or closing statements for a paragraph/passage

Topic Development (Purposeful and Focused Writing):

- Determine relevance of information to the focus of a paragraph/passage (adding/deleting sentences or phrases)
- Determine author intent (whether or not a passage has met a specific goal)

First things first, **go in order and answer the questions as you read.** This is the one section of the exam where it does not make sense to skip around. The passages and questions are of the same difficulty and style, so it's best to just go in order.

That being said, there are a **few types of questions that you may not want to answer right away**. You may get a question, for example, that asks you to select a good introduction or transition sentence. That's really not possible to answer unless you have a good idea of what you're trying to introduce or transition into, so you should read on, determine what the main idea is, and then answer the question accordingly.

Next, **you don't want to focus solely on the underlined portions of the sentence,** for multiple reasons. First, by narrowing your focus on one particular part of a sentence, you may miss a bigger error in the overall sentence structure. What may sound fine as a snippet may be problematic for the sentence as a whole. Sentence structure is a widely tested topic, so it's important that you read sentences (and your proposed corrections) **in their entirety**. We will discuss the specifics of sentence structure later on, but know that you should be mindful of this concept at all times.

> Ex: The professor <u>who researched the flight patterns of Canadian geese</u>, who become flightless for several weeks during the summer months, using advanced tracking devices.

> The phrase "the professor who researched the flight patterns of Canadian geese" doesn't necessarily register as wrong. There's no improper verb tense, pronoun usage, or punctuation – nothing that your ear will identify as being problematic. When we read the full sentence, however, we realize that there's an issue in the overall sentence structure. We have a subject (the professor), but there is no *active* verb in the sentence. The phrase "who researched the flight patterns of Canadian geese" <u>is simply describing the subject</u>. There's nothing telling us what the subject is *doing*. That would be like saying: "The car that was parked outside....." You'd think "what about the car parked outside?!" It's the same scenario here and it's our job to spot that and fix it.

Issues with sentence structure will sometimes require us to add more language; other times it will require us to remove language. You should always think:

1) **Do I have enough?**
2) **Do I have too much?**

Again, we discuss sentence structure in greater detail later.

Sometimes, the ACT will get <u>really</u> tricky and give you a mistake to fix **in hopes that you ignore a potentially bigger one** like this. Let's say they *had* used an incorrect pronoun or verb tense. Your mind thinks it's spotted the error, fixes it, and then moves on, but you still have to **make sure that the correction works for the entire sentence and that there are no bigger issues that need fixing.**

Also, **be sure you identify *specifically* what is being underlined and what language the answer choices *actually* contain**. This is another way the ACT will try to trick you, by assuming you're carelessly identifying what is actually being corrected and how.

Ex: The human resource department collected <u>more then a</u> handful of resumes from the local job fair.

The main issue here is clear; "then" should be replaced with "than." That doesn't mean you should circle the first answer you see that contains "than." You might see answer choices like these:

a) NO CHANGE

b) more than

c) at least a

d) several

You might default to selecting b) based on what you assumed your correction would entail. You would be wrong to select it. This answer choice does not contain the "a," which was included in the underlined portion of the original sentence. Anything that's underlined is up for deletion; if it belongs in the sentence – like the "a" in our example – you need to be sure that you pick an answer choice that includes it.

**Reread the sentence with your correction** to double check that it makes sense contextually and grammatically. Hearing it in your head (and even mouthing the words) will really help you to identify if something is missing.

Before we move on, let's take one more look at the previous example.

Ex: The human resource department collected <u>more then a</u> handful of resumes from the local job fair.

a) NO CHANGE

b) more than

c) at least a

d) several

If you hadn't noticed the issue with answer choice b, you may have found yourself struggling to decide between answers b and c. They both effectively illustrate the same idea in about the same number of words, so they both appear right. **That should be a red flag! We cannot have two correct answers**, so if you find that you're deciding between two "right" answer choices, you've probably missed a problem with one of the answer choices. It's also very possible that they are **both** incorrect, which leads us to our next strategy.

**Eliminate answer choices that are essentially the same**. Certain words or forms or punctuation are essentially **identical**. Sure, they are *technically* different, but they serve the exact same purpose. You will never be asked to choose stylistically between two correct options. If they can't both be right, that means they're both wrong!

The **semicolon** and the **period** are identical (at least for the purpose of the ACT). If one answer choice contains a period and the other a semicolon, and e**verything else about the answer choices is the same, <u>eliminate them both immediately.</u>**

Transition words/phrases that are synonyms of one another should also be eliminated:

- Thus = Hence = Therefore = As a result = Consequently
- However = Conversely = Contrastingly
- Nevertheless = Regardless
- Additionally = Furthermore
- Similarly = Likewise

For our next strategy, let's revisit one of our earlier examples.

> Ex: The professor <u>who researched the flight patterns of Canadian geese,</u> who become flight-less for several weeks during the summer months, using advanced tracking devices.

Our goal here is to **simplify longer/difficult sentences.** When we first talked about this example, we compared it to the statement "the car that was parked outside." It was easy to identify a mistake in the second example because it was so short. The sentences on the exam are going to be longer and more involved, so we want to look for ways that we can simplify them so that our ear can more easily identify possible mistakes.

Lifting out any non-essential information is a great place to start. Phrases that lie in between parentheses, double dashes, or double commas (although you should note that not all language between two commas is removable) are not necessary and can be removed from the sentence. We'll talk about that more when we do our punctuation lesson. If we removed the extra information enclosed between the commas from the example above, the sentence becomes much easier to absorb. It would read as:

> Ex: The professor who researched the flight patterns of Canadian geese using advanced tracking devices.

Here are some things you can do to simplify longer/difficult sentences

- **Reword longer phrases.** Instead of "scientists from Columbia University's advanced geology department and researchers from NASA's aerospace training division," rephrase the statement as "group A and group B."

- **Remove unnecessary information.** That includes non-essential, descriptive information (like we saw in the example above), dependent clauses, and transitional words

- **Replace difficult or fancy language** with words you're more familiar with. If you recognize a word or phrase, but it's not something you would use in everyday language, replace it with language you would regularly use.

..................................................................................................................

Lastly, **don't forget about the bigger picture**. Writing needs to be grammatically correct, but it also needs to be <u>purposeful</u>. The whole point of language is conveying meaning to illustrate an idea, so you want to pick words, phrases, and entire sentences that **emphasize the main idea being discussed**. That's another reason why we don't want to focus solely on the underlined portions of sentences or even just on the sentences that contain possible corrections. There are going to be plenty of sentences that are not subject to corrections, but you should still be reading them! If you don't, you'll miss out on a lot of contextual information. You don't need to read *too* carefully, but you'll want to know what the overall point and structure of the passage is.

This is especially helpful for author intent questions, which are very often the last question of a passage and ask if an author has satisfied a certain purpose. To answer this effectively, you have to know what the passage is about. You won't have that understanding if you ignore entire pieces of writing. If you are still a little unsure about what the passage's main idea is, don't reread the entire thing: **reread the title, briefly skim through the intro/conclusion, and read the topic and closing sentences of each paragraph**. This will give you a pretty good idea of what the passage was about and help you decide whether or not an author fulfilled some sort of requirement as expressed in any given question.

..................................................................................................................

Now that we have a better idea of how to tackle the English section as a whole, let's discuss some strategies for specific types of questions, namely, those dealing with punctuation, verb tense, and sentence structure. These are topics we will be reviewing in greater depth later on. If you feel these are weak areas for you, you may want to skip ahead to review these concepts before focusing on the strategies.

For starters, **know your rules for punctuation**. There are a lot of questions you can rely on your ear for, but punctuation shouldn't be one of them. Instincts aren't enough, so make sure you really solidify the actual rules of punctuation.

This is especially important for commas. For the purpose of the ACT, there are five major reasons for using a comma. Those reasons should really guide your comma usage. It can be tempting to say "I would take a natural pause when saying this sentence, so I must need a comma," but you should only use commas when there is a <u>legitimate purpose</u> for it. Placing it into one of those five categories will help you determine if a comma is legitimately usable or not. You don't want to get fooled into placing punctuation where it doesn't belong. Even if there's a lot of text, that doesn't mean a comma is necessary. Generally, **less is more when it comes to commas** on the exam.

This is another reason why simplifying sentences is useful. Earlier, we talked about shortening phrases like "scientists from Columbia University's advanced geology department and researchers from NASA's aerospace training division," into "group A and group B." We mostly did that so that the sentence was mentally easier to digest, but it's also a good technique for comma placement. If we wouldn't put a comma between "group A and group B," we don't need one in the longer example, even though it contains significantly more language.

We also spoke about lifting out non-essential information as a means of simplifying longer sentences; this has a direct relationship to comma usage. Additional information commas are often seen in pairs for the purpose of interjecting extra information into the middle of a sentence. The extra information is not necessary for grammar, sentence structure, or context. **If we're ever unsure if we have a situation that calls for the double commas, we can lift out the information between the commas and see if the sentence still makes sense.** If the sentence does not require the information in question, we will surround the language with double commas.

This is especially useful with names. It can be really hard to determine if someone's name is necessary or not, so use the removal trick to read the sentence without the name. If the sentence does not make sense that means the name is essential and we don't require commas. If the sentence works well without the name, the name is considered non-essential and we will "hug" it with the double commas.

> Ex: When marine biologist Rebecca Martinez used small satellite trackers to follow the motion of wild sea turtles, she was surprised to find that hatchlings were fairly quick and adequate swimmers.

> Here, the sentence would not make sense if we removed the name "Rebecca Martinez." Because her name is essential both grammatically and contextually, no commas are necessary. **We do not like to separate a person's job, title, or role from their actual name**, so an answer choice that contained "marine biologist, Rebecca Martinez" would not be correct. These are the answer choices you would have likely encountered:

> a) NO CHANGE
>
> b) marine biologist, Rebecca Martinez,
>
> c) marine biologist, Rebecca Martinez
>
> d) marine biologist Rebecca Martinez,

Typically answers with two commas surrounding the name (like we see in choice b) or answers with no commas (like we see in choice a) are the correct answers. Answers with the comma in between the name and the job/title/role (as we see in choice c) are never correct. Answers with a single comma at the end (like we see in choice d) are rarely correct.

Again, we will discuss in detail the rules for commas and all forms of punctuation later on. Make sure to review those rules and refer back to them on the exam. The ACT recognizes the most common misconceptions with punctuation rules and fills the exam with traps. If you know the rules very well, you're less likely to fall for these tricks.

Let's talk about one grammar concept for which you *can* rely on your ear: subject verb agreement. Errors in subject-verb agreement don't happen often in everyday speech, so they're pretty easy to spot. You wouldn't say "the book are heavy" or "the boys loves going skiing." The problem is, once again, that you will be dealing with much longer and trickier sentences. The ACT will use that to its advantage; it will place a lot of language between the subject and the verb so that your ear is less likely to pick up on any mistakes.

Luckily, there's a simple fix: **identify the subject and read it directly next to the active verb**. The subject is the specific noun performing the action in the sentence. It is **NOT** always the noun that appears just before the verb. It's typically one of the earlier nouns in a sentence.

> Ex: The exercise demonstrated by the skilled instructors, who each worked as chiropractors for the surrounding communities, <u>were difficult</u> to master.

> The verb in question here is "were." To determine if this is the proper tense, we need to find our subject. There are several nouns in the sentence that can easily throw us off track, but the actual subject is "the exercise." If we read the subject directly next to the active verb, we will spot the error immediately. "The exercise were difficult" is clearly not correct.

> The sentence contained several plural nouns before the verb "were" that tricks the ear into thinking there are no issues. Carefully identifying which noun was the actual subject completing the action was crucial.

Questions dealing with subject-verb agreement can make excellent use of our next strategy: **when in doubt, pick the answer that is the least like the other three.** You might be familiar with the jingle **"One of these things is not like the others."** That sort of thinking can really help you when all else fails. For verb tense questions, if three answer choices line up with a singular verb, and only one lines up with a plural verb, it's likely that the unique choice is the correct one.

| SINGULAR SUBJECT (she, the book, etc.) | PLURAL SUBJECT (they, the cars, etc.) |
|---|---|
| is | are |
| was | were |
| has | have |
| Verb that ends in "s" | Verb that does NOT end in "s" |

Circling back to our example, here are some choices you may have seen.

Ex: The exercise demonstrated by the skilled instructors, who each worked as chiropractors for the surrounding communities, <u>were difficult</u> to master.

    a) NO CHANGE
    b) have been difficult
    c) was difficult
    d) are difficult

Answers (a), (b), and (d) would all work for a PLURAL subject. The verbs "were" and "are" and the helping verb "have" would all pair with a plural subject. The verb "was" is the only option that would pair with a SINGULAR subject. That is our correct answer choice; it pairs with the subject of the sentence: the exercise.

If you had misidentified the subject and assumed it was the "instructors" or "communities" that needed to be paired with the verb, you may have thought to yourself that "were difficult," "are difficult," and even "have been difficult" all sounded fine.

**Remember, that should be a red flag! We can't have two (or three) correct answers!** Do not just circle the one that you "like" the best.

........................................................................................................

Many of the questions on the ACT don't have much to do with grammar rules at all, but rather deal with the notion of **clear, concise, non-redundant, and purposeful writing.** These questions test your ability to <u>edit</u> writing so that it is effective in building an overall argument. This may seem subjective, but **the ACT will have its own set of rules to apply to writing.** Once you become familiar with these "rules," identifying the correct answer will become much simpler.

Let's start with one of the most important rules of all: **concise is nice. <u>Very often, the shortest answer choice is the most effective</u>.** If more language is required for **clarity** or **grammatical** reasons, a longer answer choice might be necessary. We want to keep extra language if that language provides <u>clarity, relevant detail, or language that's necessary for grammatical reasons</u>. For example, we can't use a short pronoun like "it" if it's not clear what "it" is referring to, so sometimes more language is necessary. But if it's **clear** what's being said and the sentence is structurally sound, **the ACT will always favor something with fewer words.**

It's not just wordiness that shorter answers help to fix. Shorter answer choices will also indicate that you may need to search for **redundancies. If one answer choice is significantly shorter than the rest (or the exam gives you the option to delete/omit language), you want to search carefully for redundancies.** <u>If information has already been stated, you don't need it.</u> The redundant information isn't always nearby. Sometimes the repeated information is a detail that was given sentences or even paragraphs away. Don't get tricked into thinking that repetitive information is necessary for emphasis. Remember to think about the "rules" for the ACT: they will always favor the choice that relays the necessary information as concisely as possible.

> Ex: In 1849, Monterey – located on the coastline of Central California – became the state's first official capital. Several diplomats from the surrounding areas met <u>in the mid 1800's in</u> Monterey to sign California's first constitution after months of careful consideration and discussions.

a) NO CHANGE

b) in the coastal city of

c) following lengthy deliberations in

d) DELETE the underlined portion

All of these answer choices are grammatically correct and we were not presented with a question that asked us to include a specific *type* of detail. That means an argument can be made for more than one of these answers, which is a problem!

But there is a bigger issue with these answer choices, and choice (d) gives us a big clue as to what that problem is: redundancies. The phrase "in the mid 1800's," although informative, is completely unnecessary. We already specified in the sentence before that this event took place in 1849. The phrase "in the coastal city of" is also repeating information found in the preceding sentence. The phrase "following lengthy deliberations" is essentially rephrasing the language found later in the sentence, which specifies that the event occurred after months of discussions. Although none of these phrases were *identical* to the information found nearby, they are all illustrating points that have already been made.

...................................................................................................................................

The next few strategies will all deal with word choice and idioms. Word choice problems will require you to select <u>the most appropriate term for a given situation</u>. You will need to select the word with the correct meaning/spelling and the one that matches the author's tone.

Unfortunately, some of these questions will come down to luck. You may not recognize all of the possible words or know which spelling is accurate. Selecting between cite and site, allusion and illusion, and conscious and conscience are a few examples of questions that have appeared on exams, but they are nearly impossible to prepare for. Memorizing hundreds of vocabulary words is not an effective way to prepare, so we will simply need to rely on some other skills and memorize the meanings/spellings of the words that DO appear regularly. These include:

- Then vs. than
- Affect vs. effect
- Fewer vs. less

Note: we will discuss these all later in greater detail.

Generally, **you will want to avoid casual or conversational language** and pick phrases that are more formal. If you have the choice between "a bunch of" and "several," you should absolutely select "several."

It's also crucial that you **know the difference between informal speech and written grammar**. <u>The way we speak and the way we write are different</u>, so you can't rely strictly on how something sounds. One of the most common mistakes occurs with the phrases "would have," "could have," and "should have." When spoken, most will use the contraction "would've," which sounds a whole lot like "would *of*." The latter is <u>completely incorrect</u>, which is proof that we cannot rely solely on our ears for questions of this nature.

**Do not default to selecting a word *just* because it's familiar to you**<u>.</u> If your instinct tells you it doesn't belong in the specific sentence, use that as a reason to eliminate it. It's safer to select an unknown word than a word that is familiar but that doesn't work for the given situation.

> Ex: The measuring devices were deemed ineffective. After a follow-up study was performed, it was determined that the original findings were <u>deceitful</u>.

>> a) NO CHANGE
>> b) erroneous
>> c) insincere
>> d) wacky

We'll make use of a couple of the strategies we have discussed so far. The first answer choice we can eliminate is "wacky," as it is far too informal/conversational. Contextual clues from the sentence before and the underlying pattern in our answer choices help us understand that the sentence is trying to indicate that the findings were **wrong**.

We must be picky with our answer choices, however. Words like "deceitful" and "insincere" are both typically used to characterize a *person*, and they both indicate that the errors were *intentional*. This situation does not call for that. That means we are left to pick a word that we may not have recognized, but that's okay! We can make a solid argument against the other choices, so it's a pretty safe bet to choose "erroneous," which means false.

Minor differences in the answer choices are incredibly important for questions like these. **Some words can be used as synonyms in certain situations, but not in others.** Words like "wrong" and "unethical" can be used interchangeably if we are discussing actions that are immoral or corrupt. We can call a politician's decision to lie to the public "wrong" or "unethical." However, we can't use both of these words in *all* situations. We can say that the statement "2 + 2= 5" is "wrong," but we wouldn't be able to say it is "unethical." When it comes to word choice, <u>it will always come down to the specific situation</u>, and that's what must be considered.

...................................................................................................................

Idiom-based questions, like vocabulary questions, will sometimes come down to luck in the sense you may or may not recognize the given phrase. Idioms are peculiar phrases in English that culturally develop over time but wouldn't make much sense to you if English wasn't your native language. A phrase like "cold feet," for example, indicates that someone is nervous; it does not mean that their actual feet are chilly! Don't worry too much about questions like these. They will never account for too many questions on a single exam and it does not make sense to attempt memorizing dozens of idioms.

........................................................................................................................................................

One type of word choice problem that *will* account for several questions and that we can prepare for are transitional words. **Transition words/phrases** – ones like "however," "additionally," "for example," "nevertheless" – are an important topic on the ACT. These words help to <u>emphasize some sort of relationship</u> between two thoughts (often between a sentence and the sentence before or after). To select a proper transition word, you must **determine what that relationship is.** Follow these steps:

1) Reread the sentence before and/or after and paraphrase what it's about

2) Reread the sentence containing the question **without the transition word already provided.** Many times, the transition word that's already there is not correct, which will tend to warp your idea of what's being said. Reading the sentence without the current word/phrase gives you a clean slate. Paraphrase what this sentence is about.

3) Determine what type of relationship exists between these two statements. There are a handful of relationships that you might run into, but the most common are the following:

   a) Cause and effect

   b) Contrast

   c) Addition

   d) Similarity

   e) Illustration

4) If it's difficult to determine which type of relationship you have (and by extension, what word/phrase to select), rely on some of your basic test taking strategies. **Eliminate synonyms and/or any answer choices that you are certain do NOT work for this situation.**

Let's discuss the common relationships in greater detail.

**Cause and Effect:** when the second statement is a **result** of the first. Common transition words/phrases for this relationship are:

- As a result
- Thus
- Hence

- Therefore
- Consequently (this does NOT have a negative connotation)

**Contrast**: when two **strikingly different** thoughts are presented next to each other. Common transition words/phrases for this relationship are:

- However
- Conversely
- In contrast
- On the other hand (often following "on one hand")
- Whereas
- Despite
- Nevertheless
- Regardless
- Even so

  Note: Some of these have *slightly* different meanings.

**Addition**: when new information is presented to reinforce an idea. Common transition words/phrases for this relationship are:

- Additionally
- Furthermore
- Moreover
- Also

**Similarity**: when <u>closely related</u> ideas are used to express agreement or emphasize an idea. Common transition words/phrases for this relationship are:

- Similarly
- Likewise

**Illustration**: when specific details/instances are used to support the preceding statement. Common transition words/phrases for this relationship are:

- For example
- For instance
- Namely

Some less common relationships you may also run into:

**Summary** (to wrap up or rephrase an idea): in short, in other words, in summary

**Order** (to define some element of time/chronology): Lastly, finally, firstly, then

**Emphasis** (to indicate importance): indeed, in fact

Be detail-oriented when it comes to selecting transitional words. Illustration, addition, and similarity are all relationships that agree with or continue an argument, so they can be difficult to differentiate.

> Ex: Following the hurricane that devastated the coastal cities, several cases of looting and home break-ins were being reported. <u>However,</u> instances of assault and other violent crimes saw a surge in the aftermath of the storm.

> a) NO CHANGE
>
> b) For example,
>
> c) Conversely,
>
> d) Additionally

Let's work through our steps:

1) The first sentence is discussing the increase in crimes (robbery related) following a hurricane.

2) The second sentence is discussing the increase in violent crimes following the hurricane.

3) The second sentence is providing extra information that ties into the discussion begun in the first sentence. For that reason, "additionally" is a great option.

4) If we weren't convinced that "additionally" is the proper choice, we could start eliminating the incorrect/repetitive options. "Conversely" and "however" are synonyms of one another, so we can eliminate them both. They also don't make any sense in this context given that there is no contrast between the two statements. "For example" also does not make sense for this situation. Although our sentences are working together to support an argument, the second statement is NOT an example of what was discussed in the first sentence.

> Our correct answer, then, is "additionally."

It's possible that none of the transition words will apply to the situation you're given; in that case, you'll have the option of not including any transition words. That's perfectly fine! Do not feel forced into selecting a transition that doesn't belong.

......................................................................................................

Let's now discuss rhetorical writing skills on a larger scale. These types of questions will not require you to select the proper grammar, but rather the proper **content**. Once again, you will be forced to consider the bigger picture and edit the text so that it is **clear and purposeful**. You may see questions that require you to:

1) Select entire sentences or phrases
2) Order or place sentences or paragraphs
3) Delete or add possible sentences or phrases

Let's start with the most important strategy of all: **pay attention to the question**! Several problems on the grammar section don't appear with actual questions, but **if there *is* a physical question, read it <u>carefully</u> and <u>circle the key words</u>**. All of the answer choices are going to be grammatically correct and somewhat relevant, but you want to select the answer choice that <u>satisfies whatever conditions they've given you</u>.

If they ask for the most descriptive sentence, choose the one with the most descriptive language. If they ask for the sentence with the most specific detail, choose an answer choice with stronger, more precise language. We can't rely on eliminating answer choices that are "incorrect" in the grammatical sense, so you have to pay close attention to what it is the ACT is asking you to do.

Ex: The teacher reviewed the paper <u>for several minutes</u> before determining that the student had plagiarized a portion of the essay.

Which choice most specifically emphasizes the extreme extent to which the teacher reviewed the document?

a) NO CHANGE
b) intensely
c) for some time
d) with painstaking detail for almost an hour

The phrases we should be paying close attention to in the question are "specifically emphasizes," and "extreme extent." With those in mind, it is clear that answer choice (d) is our best option. While the other answer choices were grammatically correct and/or dealt with *part* of the question prompt, only this answer choice gives us the most <u>specific details</u> (indicating it was almost an hour and not merely "several minutes" or "some time") and <u>bold language</u> that highlights the effort level of the teacher (with the phrase "painstaking detail"). An answer choice like "intensely" does illustrate some level of extremity, but does not contain any specific details.

If you come across a content question like this and you are completely stuck, **choose the one that is the least like the other 3**. It's possible that because the answer choice deviates in some way from all the others that it is the only one that actually answers the question.

You will often be asked to select/edit entire sentences, very often either introductions, conclusions, or transitions. We touched on this briefly when we were discussing some more general strategies, but let's discuss this in greater detail. As a reminder, **we cannot answer these questions without reading the surrounding information**.

- For **introductions**, we will want to read ahead, determine what the paragraph's main idea is, and select a statement that relates to that information.

- For **conclusions**, we will want to reread the paragraph before, determine its main idea, and select a statement that wraps up that discussion

  - If asked to conclude the **entire passage** , determine the passage's <u>main idea</u> by rereading the title, introduction, and first and last line of each paragraph

- For **transitions**, we will want to skim <u>both the paragraph before</u> **and** <u>after</u>, determine the main idea of each, and select a statement that bridges those two ideas together.

    Ex:

    With a matter of weeks until the election, Senator Myers was doing all that she could to boost her approval ratings. She attended several national events for veterans and underprivileged communities, and helped to raise funds for a number of highly regarded charities.

    <u>The vote was scheduled to take place on September 15th, just weeks before her 55th birthday.</u> Voters found her to be unauthentic and opportunistic. Focus groups described her philanthropic endeavors as "mere photo ops that lacked true empathy or compassion for the American people." Uncertain that they would be able to regain momentum, Meyer's campaign manager resigned unexpectedly.

    Given all the answers are true, pick the one that provides the most effective transition.

    a) NO CHANGE
    b) Meyers grew up in Oregon, where she would be finishing up the final days of her campaign tour.
    c) Despite these efforts, the American people were not impressed.
    d) Some of the charities she worked with included the National Alliance to End Homelessness and The Global Fund for Women.

To select a proper transition, the sentence should somehow bridge the gap between the information that came before it and the information that follows. It's also crucial that **any** sentence addition (transitional or otherwise) contains information **relevant at <u>this</u> point in the passage.** Information that is loosely related to the subject is never correct. While answer choices (a) and (b) both provide information about Meyers and/or the election, they are not pinpointing the main ideas of these two paragraphs.

The first paragraph talks about Meyer's efforts to gain approval with the population through various means. The next paragraph goes on to discuss the issues she encountered. While answer choice (d) focuses on what information came before (by further describing the involvement in charities), it does nothing to introduce the information that follows. Answer choice (c) perfectly connects the two paragraphs by referencing the efforts discussed in the previous paragraph and then highlighting the problems discussed in the following sentences.

........................................................................................................................................................

Another content-based question you will encounter are sentence addition/deletion questions. For these, you will be asked whether or not a phrase or entire sentence should be included in the passage. There are two major things to keep in mind for questions like these: relevance and flow. Sentences should be added/kept when they:

- Provide relevant detail for the argument being made at this point in the passage
- Provide explanatory or clarifying information not found elsewhere (remember, we don't like redundancy)
- Do not disrupt the conversation

Relevance can be tricky here; it's not enough that the information be relevant to the passage as a whole. **It must be relevant at this specific point in the passage**. Read a few sentences before and after the potential line addition, determine what is being discussed, and decide whether or not this information would **help to build towards the argument**. That means it can't be loosely relevant. Providing a random fact, even if it has some connection to the information in the paragraph, is not necessary. **It has to emphasize the main point.** If it does, we will keep/insert it.

If it does not provide something of significant relevance or it **disrupts the flow of the paragraph**, we will delete/omit it. Interrupting the current discussion is just as problematic as being irrelevant.

Thinking about *purpose and order* should help you decide whether a statement belongs, but that's only half the battle. Each answer choice will also contain a justification to support your decision. **Read the justifications carefully and in their entirety.** It can be easy to only focus on the "yes/no" part of the question and skim through the justifications, but that will very often get you into trouble. Several of the justifications are wholly or partly untrue.

The good news is you can use that to your advantage! If you're having difficulty determining whether or not something should be added or deleted, focus on the justifications and eliminate the ones that are wrong.

After some practice, you will start to recognize the type of language that is often found in the proper justifications. Many times when we delete something, it's because the statement distracts the reader or blurs the focus of the paragraph, so you will see words like "blurs," "disrupts," and "distracts" in the justifications. Again, make sure the justifications are *entirely* true; many of them are designed to trick you. It's not enough to say the sentence is a distraction; be precise with the language. What *exactly* is it a distraction from?

Ex:

The chances of a diagnosis were slim [1]. Specialists from around the world were called upon to provide any insights they may have, but doctors still struggled to find a solution.

The author is considering adding the following statement at point [1]. Should they make this addition?

,with fewer than .05% of the hospital's cases reporting similar symptoms.

a) Yes, because it explains the procedure doctors use to make proper diagnoses.

b) Yes, because it specifically illustrates why the diagnosis was difficult and emphasizes how dire the situation was

c) No, because it does not adequately explain which type of specialists were contacted.

d) No, because it undermines the central claim of the paragraph

The given information provides specific details that are relevant to the argument being made. For this reason, the addition should be made. That narrows it down to choices (a) and (b), but it's important that we now properly determine **precisely** what the information tells us. It does not explain in any way *how* diagnoses are made, so answer choice (a) can be eliminated.

Even if we couldn't determine whether or not the extra information belonged, focusing on the justifications alone can help us arrive at the correct answer. We have already discussed why the justification for (a) is not accurate. Answer (c) uses a justification that does not make any logical sense, as the sentence in question is not focused on the specialists. Answer (d) claims that the statement undermines the central argument, which is not true. To undermine something means to weaken the argument, and if anything, this phrase helps to *support* the argument even further. That would leave us with (b) by default.

..............................................................................................................................

The final thing we are going to discuss is sentence placement and ordering. You may be asked to determine where in a paragraph or where in the passage a statement should be added. For these questions, **try to establish a relationship between the sentence and another sentence in the paragraph/passage.** Direct references, transition words, or some element of time can help place a sentence.

- If the sentence opens with a phrase like "These studies proved...," we need to place this sentence **after** those specific studies have been introduced.

- If the statement starts with a transition word like "However," we need to place it after a sentence that would **contrast** with this one.

If we don't have an obvious link to another sentence in the paragraph (or passage), we will simply want to place the statement based on what makes sense chronologically. We also want to be sure that we are **not being disruptive**. We spoke earlier about avoiding disruptions to existing conversations; that same concept should be applied to these questions.

Ex.

[1] Jericho's county fair was attracting thousands of tourists from the neighboring counties. [2] Citizens came pouring into Jericho to play games, enjoy locally sourced food, and take a ride on what local newspapers called "the Ferris wheel to end all Ferris wheels." [3] Taking these figures into account, city council members decided to add a second fair later in the year. [4] Standing 350 feet high, the Ferris wheel could be spotted for miles, welcoming travelers from all directions. [5] The fair's total revenue was estimated at 1.2 million dollars, bringing a much needed boost to the local economy.

For the sake of logic and cohesion, sentence [3] should be placed:

a) Where it is now
b) Before sentence 1
c) After sentence 4
d) After sentence 5

You may have recognized that sentence 3 felt out of place when you first read through the paragraph. For starters, it is disrupting the conversation about the Ferris wheel; sentence 2 should lead right into sentence 4.

Sentence 3 also contains a direct reference to something: the figures. That means this sentence should be placed after figures have been introduced, which occurs in sentence 5. So we will place sentence 3 after sentence 5.

........................................................................................................................

Occasionally, you will be asked to arrange multiple sentences within a paragraph. The same rules apply: arrange the sentences in a way that **flows and makes sense chronologically.** Make sure you structure the language so that people/things are being introduced **before** they are discussed in greater detail. Do not disrupt sentences that flow from one to another.

Ex:

[1] The hurricane devastated much of the Louisiana Coast and left local legislators scrambling for solutions. [2] Anything from canned goods to blankets to toilet paper were donated on behalf of the families in need. [3] Local councilwoman Laura Mackey was one of the first to organize a massive collection and distribution of supplies.

Which sequence of sentences makes this paragraph the most logical?
a) NO CHANGE

b) 1, 3, 2

c) 2, 1, 3

d) 3, 1, 2

Once again, we are simply looking to arrange the sentences in a way that makes logical sense. Sentence 1 is a broad statement about the effects of the hurricane and local officials' attempts to respond. Sentence 3 references a specific official who responded by organizing a redistribution of supplies. It makes sense to place sentence 3 after sentence 1. Sentence 2 describes the specific types of supplies that were being redistributed. So it makes sense to place sentence 2 after sentence 3 (where the supplies were first introduced).

Therefore, choice (b) is our best option. Our ideas narrowed in focus – from legislators' efforts, to a specific legislator's plan, to the details of that plan – which is exactly what we want.

.........................................................................................................................................

Before we move onto the rules for punctuation, grammar, and sentence structure, let's wrap up our discussion of English strategies by revisiting one of our general test-taking strategies: **categorizing the questions**. Determining what concept is at the root of each question helps you figure out exactly what to look for in the answer choices and what potential traps to avoid. It's usually pretty easy to identify when a question is dealing with punctuation, verb tense, or word choice based on the answer choices. Questions that appear with physical question prompts (sentence placement, sentence addition/deletion, author intent, etc.) are also easy to categorize.

As we discussed earlier, we can generally assume that wordiness and/or redundancy is being tested when one answer choice is significantly shorter than the rest or we're given the option to delete language. When it's not quite obvious what's going on, it's probably an issue of sentence structure. There is a section in our upcoming English review that deals with all of the possible issues with sentence structure (parallelism, misplaced modifiers, run-ons, comma splices, fragments). You should pay close attention to all of these elements when you believe that sentence structure is the root of the problem.

## COMMAS

It can be tempting to try and use your instincts for comma questions by "hearing" where natural pauses in a sentence may occur. You'll want to rely more on the actual rules for commas so that you are not tricked into adding commas where they don't belong. A large amount of text does not always call for a comma, so it is important to know the specific reasons why commas are utilized. Here are the 5 major reasons:

### 1)  Joining two independent clauses WITH a coordinating conjunction

In other words, when you have two complete sentences and want to combine them with a "connecting" word.

- The acronym FANBOYS may help you remember the possible coordinating conjunctions: For, And, Nor, But, Or, Yet, So

    Ex: The student could spend his time reading, but he would rather be playing video games. √

"The student could spend his time reading" and "He would rather be playing video games" are both complete sentences, so the comma used **with** the conjunction "but" is necessary to combine the two clauses.

Note: Sometimes the ACT will combine two independent clauses with a comma but NOT include a coordinating conjunction. Do not fall for their tricks! This is called a **comma splice** and is grammatically incorrect. You need a comma **AND** a coordinating conjunction.

    Ex: David went to the store, he purchased many items. ✗

This is INCORRECT as there is no coordinating conjunction between the two independent statements.

### 2)  Separating nouns/actions in a list or multiple non-essential modifiers

This is probably the type of comma you are the most comfortable and familiar with. We use it to separate multiple items, actions, or phrases.

    Ex: My three favorite fruits are apples, bananas, and strawberries. √

    Ex: Maria is going to clean her room, do her laundry, and finish her homework. √

We also use it to separate multiple non-essential modifiers. It's important to distinguish between essential and non-essential identifiers. **If you can change the order of the adjectives, they are non-essential and will require commas.**

Ex: Sophie was a brave, enthusiastic patient. ✓

Here, "brave" and "enthusiastic" are interchangeable and therefore **non-essential**. The sentence would still make sense if it was written as: Sophie was an enthusiastic, brave patient.

In some sentences, descriptive words or phrases are **essential** and belong next to the noun.

Ex: Julia was asked to read over Dylan's detailed history notes. ✓

Here, "history" is describing the TYPE of notes and "detailed" is our non-essential adjective. It would not make sense to write it as: Julia was asked to read over Dylan's history detailed notes. So we do not need a comma.

You can also **use the "and" trick** to help you with questions of this nature. **If you can place an "and" in between your descriptive words, you will need a comma.**

Ex: Sophie was a brave and enthusiastic patient. ✓

Sophie was a brave, enthusiastic patient. ✓

Note: We do NOT need a comma after the final adjective. We only add commas BETWEEN our adjectives.

Ex: Sophie was a brave, enthusiastic, patient. ✗

Remember, **less is more when it comes to commas.** This is especially true for these types of comma questions.

### 3) Transition words or phrases

Selecting the proper transition word or phrase is something we have already discussed, but now it's important we understand how to punctuate them. Commas are needed to separate these words from the rest of the sentence, whether they appear at either the beginning, end, or middle of a sentence.

If they appear at the beginning of a sentence, we use a comma after the word or phrase. If they appear at the end of a sentence, we use a comma before the word or phrase.

Ex: However, many of the students did not complete the assignment. ✓

Ex: Many of the students did not complete the assignment, however. ✓

If they appear in the middle of a sentence, we "hug" the transition word/phrase with double commas.

Ex: The students, however, were unwilling to accept the amount of work that had been assigned to them. ✓

## 4) Opening a sentence with a dependent clause

Let's start by discussing what a dependent clause is. A dependent clause is simply something that can't stand alone. It ***depends*** on an independent clause to make sense. Many times, dependent clauses will contain subordinating conjunctions like "while," "during," "since," or other indications that the information relies on another statement to make sense.

"While Jessica was reading" cannot stand alone. Even though "Jessica was reading" is a complete sentence, the "while" requires us to have more information for the sentence to actually mean anything. That information is the **independent clause**, which can appear at the beginning or end of the overall sentence. **If the independent clause appears at the beginning and is followed by the dependent clause, we don't require any punctuation.**

Ex: Nicholas was watching television while Jessica was reading. ✓

**If we restructure the sentence so that the dependent clause comes <u>FIRST</u>, we need to separate the dependent clause and independent clause with a comma.**

Ex: While Jessica was reading, Nicholas was watching television. ✓

Not all dependent clauses will contain those subordinating conjunctions, but it will be clear that the statements cannot stand on their own.

Ex: Fearful of roller coasters, Emily rejected David's invitation to go to Six Flags. ✓

## 5) Additional information

Commas are used to add **non-essential** phrases or clauses to a sentence. This can be done two ways: in the middle of a sentence or at the beginning/end of a sentence.

When the additional information is added to the end of a sentence, we simply add a comma before the non-essential phrase. When the additional information is added at the beginning of a sentence, we simply add a comma after the non-essential phrase.

Ex: Tourists flocked to the newly constructed stadium, located just north of the expressway. ✓

......................................................................................................................

When the information is **interjected** into the **middle** of a sentence, we "hug" that information with double commas. It is easy to tell when we have this scenario because **we can remove that information** and the sentence will still make sense and be grammatically correct.

Ex: The stadium, located just north of the expressway, was attracting hundreds of tourists per week. ✓

If we removed the phrase "located just north of the expressway," the sentence would read as: The stadium was attracting hundreds of tourists per week. Because this statement is grammatically correct and understandable, we know the additional information can be enclosed by the double commas.

Note: This process of figuring out whether information is essential or not (and whether or not commas are needed as a result) is especially difficult with names. Remember to ask yourself whether or not you NEED the name for the sentence to make sense.

Ex: Astronaut Neil Armstrong was the first man to walk on the moon. ✓

Here, Neil Armstrong's name is **necessary** to understand the sentence. As it is essential, we **do not section it off with commas**.

Ex: An astronaut, Bethenny Samstein, visited the high school to discuss space camp with the student body. ✓

Here, the name of the astronaut is **not necessary** grammatically or contextually. Because it is non-essential, we **surround the name with the double commas.**

## DASHES AND PARENTHESES

Dashes and parentheses are both used to insert additional/explanatory information into a sentence.

**Dashes** can be used in a very similar way that commas are used to insert additional information, in that they can be **used in pairs** to interject a statement into the **middle** of a sentence or **alone** at the **end** of a sentence.

The main difference between dashes and commas is that the information between the dashes is often more abrupt. It can disrupt the flow of the original sentence. Sometimes the statement between the dashes is its own sentence!

Ex: She read so slowly—English was her second language—that her teacher suggested she hire a tutor. ✓

Just like the double commas, **we can remove the information** between the dashes and the sentence will make sense.

We can also use a single dash at the end of a sentence to provide extra information.

Ex: The woman demanded two things from her children—appreciation and respect. ✓

The ACT will never make you choose stylistically between dashes and commas. They **will** try to trick you into selecting answer choices that contain one comma and one dash, which is **NOT** correct. You will hug additional information with either TWO commas or TWO dashes, never a mixture of the two!

**Parentheses** are used to enclose explanatory information. The ACT will mostly test you on **where** a parenthetical statement belongs. Your job is to place this information directly after the thing it is describing.

> Ex: Scientists discovered several new celestial objects using a government funded telescope and an advanced data processing system (natural objects located outside Earth's atmosphere). ✗

This is **NOT** a correct use of the parentheses. The information enclosed is meant to define a celestial object, so it should be placed directly after that term.

> Ex: Scientists discovered several new celestial objects (natural objects located outside Earth's atmosphere) using a government funded telescope and an advanced data processing system. ✓

## SEMICOLONS

**Semicolons** are sometimes referred to as a "weak period." Grammatically, **they do the same thing that** periods do: separate two independent sentences. A semicolon is used when the two thoughts are very closely related, but the ACT will never make you decide stylistically between semicolons and periods.

**Remember, that means if you see them both, you can eliminate them both!** They can't both be right!

If you're not sure if a semicolon belongs in a sentence, read it with a period and see if both sentences can stand on their own.

> Ex: Maria wasn't sure what she should bring to the picnic; eventually, she decided to bring brownies. ✓

Here, the semicolon is perfectly fine because it is separating two independent clauses and a period could have easily been put in its place.

> Ex: Carlos was certain he wanted to bring chips to the picnic; because they are his favorite snack. ✗

Here, the semicolon is **NOT** used properly. "Because they are his favorite snack" is not a complete sentence, so we cannot use a semicolon.

## COLONS

**Colons** are very simply used to introduce related information **after a complete sentence**. It is very important that what comes **before** the colon be an **independent clause**, but what comes **after** the colon can take **many** forms. <u>Don't be fooled into thinking that lists are the only</u> thing that can follow a colon! As long as the information provides some sort of detail or information related to the opening statement, it can be anything: a list, a word, a name, a phrase, a quote, or even another complete sentence.

     Ex: I need to purchase several ingredients to bake an apple pie: sugar, flour, and apples. ✓

Here, the three items placed after the colon specify the ingredients referenced in the opening sentence. What the colon essentially did here was **eliminate the need for language like "which are."**

Don't be fooled into picking an answer choice that contains language like "which are" or "such as" AND a colon.

     Ex: I have three favorite hobbies: which are skiing, dancing and swimming. ✗

This is **NOT** correct.

...................................................................................................................................

Colons are **not always followed by a list!** Sometimes the information will be very short and succinct, but other times the information will be lengthy, and that's okay. Don't shy away from a colon just because what follows it is a longer phrase or complete sentence.

     Ex: Jared loved the artistry in the performance: each dancer was more ornately dressed than the last. ✓

Here, the statement following the colon is a complete sentence, but as it provides specific information about the preceding statement, a colon is perfectly acceptable. The phrase **before** the colon was a complete sentence, and that is really the most important thing.

...................................................................................................................................

## POSSESSIVE APOSTROPHES

**Possessive apostrophes**, as their name suggests, are meant to indicate possession or ownership.

For **SINGULAR** nouns, you will add the apostrophe **BEFORE** the "s."

     Ex: That car's tires are flat. ✓

Because I am referencing a single car (as indicated by the word "that"), the apostrophe is placed before the "s"

For **PLURAL** nouns, you will add the apostrophe **AFTER** the "s."

      Ex: Those cars' horns are very loud. ✓

Here, I am referencing multiple cars (as indicated by the word "those"), so the apostrophe is placed after the "s."

Sometimes it will be obvious whether a noun is singular or plural based on its spelling. The word "baby," for example, changes its spelling to "babies" when it is made plural. For a word like "car," the spelling does not change so you will have to **use contextual clues** from the sentence or passage to figure out if you are talking about one or several cars.

### VERBS

When it comes to verbs, the ACT is mostly concerned with two things: **correct tense** and **subject-verb agreement.** Let's begin with verb tense. This is one concept that you can rely pretty heavily on your ear for. Verb tense is generally not something we mess up in everyday speech, so errors are fairly easy to spot.

If we want to get technical, there are six basic tenses:

**Simple present:** They swim.

**Present perfect:** The have swum.

**Simple past:** They swam.

**Past perfect:** They had swum.

**Simple future:** They will swim.

**Future perfect:** They will have swum.

Some of these tenses can be a little tricky, especially with a word like "swim," whose past tense requires more than simply adding "ed" to the end of the word.

For all the **perfect** tenses, we use what is called the **past participle**, in this case "swum." We also need to use helping words like "have/had" for the perfect tenses. Sometimes the ACT will try to trick you into choosing an incorrect version of these trickier tenses.

Ex: They have chose to see a Broadway musical. ✗

This is **NOT** correct. The verb in question here is "choose." "Chose" is its simple past tense and "chosen" is its past participle. We would not mix a simple past tense with the helping word "have." Proper sentence structures could include:

They chose to see a Broadway musical.

They have chosen to see a Broadway musical.

They had chosen to see a Broadway musical.

Figuring out which tense to use also comes down to context. You must figure out what tense the author is writing in to select the correct verbs. Looking for other verbs in the sentence and other verbs in the preceding sentences can give you some important clues about the proper tense. **In most cases, we rely heavily on consistency.**

> Ex: The teacher explained to the student that he can visit her office hours at any time and that she will be happy to help him. ✗

This sentence is **NOT** correct because it mixes the past tense (explained) with the present tense (can) and future tense (will be).

> Ex: The teacher explained to the student that he could visit her office hours at any time and that she would be happy to help him. ✓

Note: In some cases, it DOES make sense to have multiple tenses in one sentence. You'll just need to use your instincts to ensure it makes sense.

> Ex: I was invited to attend the school dance, but I think I will be vacationing that day. ✓

Here, we have several different tenses in one sentence, but the progression from past to present to future makes sense in this context.

> Ex: Next summer, I was swamped with school work. ✗

Here, the mixture of tenses does not make any sort of sense.

........................................................................................................................

One of the most commonly tested topics dealing with grammar usage is **subject-verb agreement.**

The basic concept is:

If your subject is **SINGULAR**, the verb will **END WITH AN "S".**
If your subject is **PLURAL**, the verb will **NOT END WITH AN "S".**

It is very easy to hear mistakes when this rule is broken!

> Ex: The girl walk to the store. ✗

> Ex: The boys walks to the store. ✗

**Refer back to the strategy section to locate important skills for tackling these questions.** These questions can be rather tricky, as the ACT will lay out some substantial traps that can be easy to fall into. Avoid those traps by solidifying those strategies.

........................................................................................................................

## PRONOUNS

**Pronouns** are words that we use in place of a noun or noun phrase. These are words like you, he, her, them, it, those, who, which, etc.

For the most part, your job will be making sure the pronouns **match** the nouns they are referring to and that they are **clear**. It is totally unnecessary to repeat a noun several times within one sentence (or even multiple sentences) if it is **clear** what is being referenced.

> Ex: Sally is very interested in space, so she applied for an internship at NASA. ✓

> Ex: Working at NASA had always been a dream of Sally's. She applied for an internship in the engineering program as soon as she was old enough. ✓

In both cases, the pronoun "she" is close enough to "Sally" for the reader to understand what is happening. If the noun is stated at the end of the preceding sentence, we very rarely need to start the following sentence with restatement of the noun (as you can see in the second example above.)

"She" also matches with "Sally," because Sally is a singular female noun. Make sure you figure out what noun is being described by the pronoun and that the two match. Think about:

Singular vs. plural (he vs. they)
Male vs. female (he vs. she)
Active vs. passive (he vs. him)
Human vs. object (he vs. it)

.................................................................................................................

Pronouns that do not match the noun or do not clearly indicate who/what is being talked about are incorrect.

> Ex: Paul was fighting with Steven, so he decided not to go to his birthday party. ✗

It is totally unclear who "he" and "his" are referring to, so this sentence needs clarification. Even though the ACT loves concise answer choices, sometimes the lengthier option is necessary for this purpose.

> Ex: In a rush to get out of the house, Cynthia left their keys on the kitchen counter. ✗

Here, the plural pronoun "their" does not match with "Cynthia," so this sentence is incorrect.

> Ex: Each student on campus is given a detailed itinerary describing the events they are required to attend. ✗

This one is exceptionally tricky. As reader, we understand that there are multiple students who are given itineraries, so the phrase "they are" does not strike us as incorrect. The sentence is structured, however, with the subject being "each student." This is singular, so we would use a phrase like "he or she is."

> Ex: Each student on campus is given a detailed itinerary describing the events he or she is required to attend. ✓

................................................................................................................

Be careful with "her" vs. "she." Pronouns like "I," "he," "she," "they," and "we" belong with **active** verbs. These pronouns are actually **completing the action.**

Pronouns like "me," "her," "him," "them," and "us" are **passive**. These pronouns are **having the action done *to* them.**

> Ex: **She** threw the ball to **him**. ✓

This is obvious, but thinking about active/passive pronouns can help you when things get a bit more difficult.

> Ex: The parents had dozens of questions for Nicholas and I. ✗

"I" is not the correct pronoun here. Even though the phrase "Nicholas and I" generally sounds okay, it is incorrect in this case because those two nouns are **passive**. Think of how you would answer the question: Who did the parents have dozens of questions for?

We would respond with a "me" and not an "I," so we will use "me" in the original statement.

This idea of active/passive also helps greatly when choosing between **who** and **whom**. "Who" is used in the active sense and "whom" in the passive sense. If you rephrase the statement as a question, would you answer with "he/she/they" or a "him/her/them"? If it's the first, use "who." If it's the latter, use "whom."

> Ex: Sarah, **who** threw the ball to David, was being blinded by the sun.
> Who threw the ball to David? **She** did.
>
> Ex: David, to **whom** Sarah threw the ball, was being blinded by the sun.
> Who did Sarah throw the ball to? She threw it to **him**.

................................................................................................................

Pronouns like "who," "that," "which," and "whom" are usually used to introduce some additional information about a particular noun. Again, make sure they match. "Who/whom" are used to describe people and "that/which" are used to describe things and animals.

Ex: The scientists working at New York University's research facility, which were all recent graduates of the mechanical engineering program, were working tirelessly to solve the ongoing crisis. ✗

Here, the wrong pronoun is used to further describe the scientists. Given that scientists are human beings, we would use the term "who" instead of "which."

......................................................................................................................................

Possessive pronouns are used to indicate ownership. Instead of adding an apostrophe (like we do with standard nouns), we use words like "my," "his," "its," "their," and "whose." The two most difficult – and the ones you will be tested on the most frequently – are "its" and "their."

Let's begin with "its." You will see three forms of this word on the exam.

1) Its
2) It's
3) Its'

The first (**its**) is used for **possession**.

Ex: The cat was adorable. Its tail was striped and fluffy.

The second (**it's**) is the **contraction** of the words "it is."

Ex: Make sure you wear gloves. It's very cold outside.

The third (**its'**) is a completely made up word! **Do not pick it – ever!**

Moving on to "their." You will see three forms of this word on the exam.

1) Their
2) There
3) They're

The first (**their**) indicates **possession**.

Ex. The cats were adorable. Their tails were striped and fluffy.

The second (**there**) can be used to indicate **location** or to **open a sentence.**

Ex. The books are located over there.

Ex. There are several options for diners to select from.

The third (**they're**) is the **contraction** of the words "they are."

Ex. Be careful around raccoons. They're aggressive and territorial animals.

................................................................................................

**Before you worry about which form of "its" or "their" to use, you must FIRST determine which pronoun ("it" or "they") works for the given situation.** "It" is used for singular subjects; "they" is used for plural subjects. The ACT loves to lay out traps with these types of questions.

Ex: The students voted to select <u>it's</u> new class pet. ✗

Certainly "it's" is not correct: "it is" class pet makes no sense. But changing the word to "its" gives us another problem: **a mismatching pronoun**. The subject of the sentence is the students. That is a plural subject, so "it" (and by extension, the possessive form "its") will **not match**. We would need to change the word to "their," which indicates possession **AND** matches with our subject.

................................................................................................

## WORD CHOICE AND IDIOMS

Word choice problems will require you to select the most appropriate term from a given situation. You will need to choose the option with the correct spelling/meaning and one that matches the author's tone. **Consult the strategy section to review the important skills necessary to approach these questions.** Right now, we will be reviewing the rules for some of the most common word-based questions.

**Then vs. Than**: "Then" is used to denote some element of time. "Than" is used when we are drawing a comparison.

Ex: She planned on visiting her mother and then going to the store. ✓

Ex: The student was smarter than her teacher. ✓

**Affect vs. Effect**: "Affect" is the verb (think "a" for action). "Effect" is the noun (think "e" for event).

Ex: The ongoing effects from the hurricane crippled the local economy. ✓

Ex: The vote was greatly affected by the previous night's presidential debate. ✓

**Fewer vs. Less:** Both of these words are meant to indicate a smaller amount of something. Figuring out which one to use comes down to what you are comparing. If it's something that is **countable**, use "fewer." If it is something that is **measured** or a **characteristic** of something, use "less."

Ex: I have fewer friends than you do. ✓

Ex: I have less friends than you do. ✗

The second example doesn't necessarily strike us as incorrect, so if the question is dealing with less vs. fewer, **think actively about the rule, and don't rely entirely on your ear.**

Ex: I am less skilled than my mentor. ✓

Ex: It rained much less this month than it did last month. ✓

..........................................................................................................................................

As a reminder, **idioms** are peculiar phrases in English that you may or may not be familiar with. The ACT will typically test you on verb-preposition pairs like the ones listed below:

Ex: The odds are **IN** your favor

Ex: Please refrain **FROM**

Ex: She alluded **TO**

..........................................................................................................................................

**Would/Could Have vs. Would/Could of**

A reminder that "would of" is **NOT** proper English! "**Would have**" is very often shortened to "would've" which merely *sounds* like "would **of**."

Don't get fooled into selecting answer choices based solely on how they sound when you read them allowed. Like just now! "Allowed" is not the right term. It *sounds* the same as "aloud," but has a totally different meaning from the correct word for this situation. Look out for these traps.

..........................................................................................................................................

**Into Which, From Which**

This is one of the more challenging question types, because you probably don't structure sentences this way when you write. Let's start with an example first.

Ex: The driveway **she drove into** was freshly painted. ✓

Ex: The driveway **into which she drove** was freshly painted. ✓

Typically we place words like "from" or "into" **after** a verb. But we can structure the sentence in such a way that these words come **BEFORE** the verb. We need to use words like "which" or "whom" in these cases. It may feel a little unnatural at first, but don't eliminate it as an option just because it's a bit unfamiliar. Many of the other answer choices they will provide will not contain a necessary "into" or "from" term **ANYWHERE** in the sentence. That is definitely **worse** than placing it in a spot that you don't prefer.

 Ex: The author from whom I drew my greatest inspiration was Edgar Allan Poe. √

........................................................................................................

## ADJECTIVES AND ADVERBS

Another concept you may see tested on the ACT is the use of adjectives and adverbs (typically in pairs). This is something you may be able to rely a bit on your ear for, but if we want to get technical:

**Adjectives** – modify nouns

**Adverbs** – modify verbs, adjectives, and other adverbs

Adverbs typically end in "ly" or "ily." The important thing is to pair an adverb and adjective in the correct order and to not mistakenly use an adverb as an adjective. Again, this will probably sound wrong to you when you hear it being misused, so you can rely a bit on your instincts.

 Ex: The baker had an exceptionally precise way of measuring ingredients. √

"Precise" is the adjective describing the form of measurement and "exceptionally" is the adverb modifying "precise."

 Ex: The baker had an exceptional precisely way of measuring ingredients. ✗

This sentence is not properly structured, placing an adjective in front of the adverb.

........................................................................................................

Adverbs do not need to be paired with adjectives, but it is important that they not come directly before a noun.

 Ex: The burglar creepily walked down the hallway. √

Here, the adverb is simply modifying the verb "walked."

 Ex: The amazingly performance kept audience members at the edge of their seats. ✗

Here, "amazingly" is incorrectly attempting to modify the noun "performance." If we want to indicate that the performance is amazing, we simply use the adjective "amazing."

........................................................................................................

## COMPARISONS

Comparisons can be a bit tricky when we compare a noun to something found later in the sentence. We must make sure the comparison is **complete and logical.**

> Ex: The experienced actor's level of professionalism was rivaled by the young actress hoping to make a name for herself. ✗

This sentence may not sound wrong initially, but it is. We must break it down and figure out *specifically* what we are comparing. We are not comparing the actor to the actress; we are comparing the actor's *level of professionalism* to the actress's *level of professionalism*. As the sentence is right now, we are essentially comparing a level of professionalism directly to a person. When we really think about it, that doesn't make sense! It would be wordy and unnecessary to repeat "level of professionalism," so we can use a pronoun.

> Ex: The experienced actor's level of professionalism was rivaled by **that of** the young actress hoping to make a name for herself. ✓

Make sure you choose a pronoun that matches what you are actually comparing. In this example, "level of professionalism" is single and non-human, so the pronoun "that" is sufficient in setting up the comparison.

# SENTENCE STRUCTURE

Before we discuss the potential issues with sentence structure, let's first review the makings of a complete sentence. A complete sentence requires two things: a **subject** and a **verb**. The sentence must also be a **complete thought**, which will often require additional language (like an object).

The **subject** of the sentence is the noun that is **doing** or **being** something.

The **verb** is the **action being performed** or the **state of being**.

For problem sentences, you will not always be given control over the punctuation, so you may need to alter the **language** so that it follows the rules of punctuation and grammar. You may remember from the strategy section that you should be asking yourself two things:

1) Do I have enough?
2) Do I have too much?

How to deal with either of those issues will come down to which portion of the sentence is underlined (and thereby under your control) and what your answer choices are. You may have to change/add proper punctuation, delete language, or add language.

------

## COMMA SPLICES

You may recall that a **comma splice** occurs when two independent clauses are incorrectly connected with **JUST** a comma (and **no coordinating conjunction**). We can fix this problem by transforming one independent clause into a dependent clause or modifying statement. We do this by removing the subject and/or active verb.

Ex: She grew up on a farm, she was not afraid to pet the horses. ✗

Ex: Having grown up on a farm, she was not afraid to pet the horses. ✓

Here, we changed the opening statement from a complete sentence into a modifying statement about our subject.

Ex: She sat in hours of traffic, this made her late to dinner. ✗

Ex: She sat in hours of traffic, making her late to dinner. ✓

Here, we changed the structure of the closing statement to eliminate the issue of the comma splice.

------

## RUN-ONS

**Run-ons** are created when two independent sentences are connected <u>by nothing at all</u>. Again, we will need to add, eliminate, or edit the language to avoid the error in sentence structure.

>Ex: The gingerbread cookies were fresh out of the oven they filled the house with smells of Christmas. ✗

There is often more than one way to fix an error. We just need to make sure that we don't end up creating another problem.

>Ex: The gingerbread cookies were fresh out of the oven and filled the house with smells of Christmas. ✓

>Ex: The gingerbread cookies were fresh out of the oven, filling the house with smells of Christmas. ✓

................................................................................................................

## FRAGMENTS

**Fragments** are simply <u>incomplete sentences</u>. We can change the fragment into a complete sentence by making sure that it has a subject and a verb. The sentence should also make sense entirely on its own.

>Ex: The car that was parked outside. ✗

This sentence is incomplete. Although it contains a subject (the car) and a verb (was parked), it does not contain an **active** verb. The fact that the car was parked outside merely provides us **descriptive information** about the car, but there is no **action** in the sentence. It will not make sense unless we **add** or **delete** language.

>Ex: The car was parked outside. ✓

>Ex: The car that was parked outside was stolen. ✓

Verbs, often preceded by words like "who," "which," or "that," can simply be introducing descriptive information about the subject. <u>These alone cannot make a complete sentence.</u>

................................................................................................................

## PARALLELISM

**Parallelism** is really a fancy way of saying "consistency." It is best to give the phrases or clauses within a sentence the same grammatical structure. This usually comes down to verb tense.

Ex: The student hated reading, writing, and to give oral presentations. ✗

The change in verb tense here is awkward and unnecessary. We can correct it by changing one or more of the phrases to match the others.

Ex: The student hated reading, writing, and giving oral presentations. ✓

Ex: The student hated to read, write, and give oral presentations. ✓

Either alternative is fine. The second option can be a bit more challenging when figuring out what to do with the preposition "to." We really only need one preposition, but if we see that it is being repeated earlier in the sentence, for the sake of consistency, we will repeat it for *all* the phrases.

Ex: The officer knew it was his duty **to** serve his community, **to** uphold the laws, and **to** be a model citizen for others. ✓

Ex: The officer knew it was his duty **to** serve his community, **to** uphold the laws, and be a model citizen for others. ✗

........................................................................................................................

## MISPLACED MODIFIERS

A **modifier** is a word or phrase that **describes** a noun or action in a sentence. Our job is to make sure that the modifying statement is **as close to the thing it is describing as possible.**

These statements very often open a sentence in the form of a dependent clause, so we need to **follow the comma immediately with the subject** pertaining to the modifier.

Ex: Walking home from school, the scenery and pleasant weather was the perfect way for Rebecca to decompress. ✗

This sentence, even though you can probably piece together what is being said, is technically not correct. That is precisely what makes these questions so difficult: it is not always easy to "hear" the mistake. **When the only difference in the answer choices is the order of the language, it is likely that this is the concept being tested.**

Ex: Walking home from school, Rebecca felt the scenery and pleasant weather was the perfect way to decompress. ✓

Think "who is walking home from school?" and immediately place the answer to that question after the comma.

You typically have control of the language found after the comma. If and when you have control of the language **BEFORE** the comma, choose a phrase that can **reasonably apply to whatever subject is found immediately after the comma.**

## SUMMARY

- Go in order and answer the questions as you read.

- You may need to read on to answer certain questions (like picking a good introduction or transitional phrase).

- Do not focus solely on the underlined portions of the sentence.

- Make sure that the correction works for the <u>entire sentence</u> and that there are no bigger issues that need fixing.

- Be sure you identify *specifically* what is being underlined and what language the answer choices *actually* contain.

- If two answers are "right," they're either both wrong or you've missed something.

- Eliminate answer choices that are essentially the same (like periods and semicolons).

- Simplify longer/difficult sentences (eliminate non-essential information, replace challenging words with simpler synonyms, etc.).

- Concise is nice – when in doubt, pick the shortest answer choice.

- Shorter answer choices should signal you to search for redundancies.

- Know your rules for punctuation. Don't rely solely on your ear (particularly for commas).

- When in doubt, pick the answer that's the least like the other three. This is especially helpful for subject-verb agreement questions.

- Properly identify the specific subject for questions dealing with verb tense or pronouns.

- Make sure that pronouns are sufficient.

- Avoid conversational/casual language.

- Study common word choice questions (affect vs. effect, then vs. than, its vs. it's).

- Know the difference between informal speech and written grammar.

- Make sure comparisons are logical and complete.

- For word choice questions, focus on the specific situation and which word applies. Do not select words just because they are familiar to you.

- For transition words, reread the sentence before and the sentence without the current transition word. Try to establish the relationship between those two sentences and pick an appropriate transition word. Study the commonly tested transition words.

- Pay close attention to physical questions (remember, not all the questions on this section come with actual questions). Circle the key words and figure out precisely what the question is asking for.

- For content-based questions, think about the "bigger picture." Add sentences that support the argument. Eliminate those that don't.

- Do not add sentences that are disruptive.

- Read answer justifications carefully and in their entirety.

- Pick introductions/transitions that summarize the main ideas at that specific point in the passage.

- For author intent questions, reread the title and briefly skim through the passage (focus on the intro, conclusion, and first and last sentence of each paragraph).

- For sentence placement questions, try to find a link to another sentence in the paragraph (with a transition word, a direct reference, or some element of time). Do not be disruptive.

- Categorize the questions when you can. Determine what is at the root of the question. When you're finding it difficult to categorize a question, it is likely an issue of sentence structure (parallelism, run-ons, fragments, comma splices, misplaced modifiers).

# ACT MATH

........................................................................................................................

## WHAT'S THE GIST?

The math section is the second portion of the exam. It's also the longest section. You will have **60 minutes** to complete **60 questions**. This doesn't mean you will spend exactly a minute on each question, but pacing yourself around that target is important to make sure you leave enough time for the questions near the end.

Each question is a multiple choice question with five possible answer choices. You are **allowed to use your calculator for the entire section** (phew). Later on, we will discuss the functions of the calculators and provide details about which calculators are permitted on the exam.

## WHAT CAN YOU EXPECT TO SEE?

Every exam is a bit different, but you can expect to see the following topics tested on each exam. Some of these topics are tested more frequently than others. Topics listed with a (*) typically will not account for too many questions on a single exam. They're useful topics to know, but there are others that will appear far more frequently. You'll want to focus your attention on the common topics first.

**PRE-ALGEBRA**: (roughly 12–15 questions)

- Fractions, mixed numbers, decimals, and integers
- Ratios, proportions, and percents
- Multiples and factors
- Absolute values
- One-variable linear equations
- Basic probability and counting
- Mean, median, and mode

**ELEMENTARY ALGEBRA**: (roughly 9–12 questions)

- Polynomials
- Modeling
- Factoring and quadratic equations
- Inequalities
- Exponents and square roots

## INTERMEDIATE ALGEBRA: (roughly 9–12 questions)

- Quadratic formula
- Radical and rational expressions
- Sequences
- Systems of equations
- Functions
- Polynomial roots
- Complex numbers *
- Logarithms *
- Matrices *

## COORDINATE GEOMETRY: (roughly 9–12 questions)

- Number line graphs
- Graphs of points, lines, polynomials, circles, and other curves
- Relationships between equations and graphs
- Slope
- Properties of parallel and perpendicular lines
- Distance and midpoint formulas
- Transformations *

## PLANE GEOMETRY: (roughly 12–15 questions)

- Plane figures (triangles, rectangles, parallelograms, trapezoids, circles)
- Angle properties
- Perimeter, area, and volume
- Translations, reflections, and rotations
- 3-D geometry *

## TRIGONOMETRY: (roughly 3–6 questions)

- Trigonometric functions, identities, and equations
- Right triangle trigonometric ratios *
- Trigonometric curves *

Keep in mind: The exam **does not provide you with a formula sheet**, so you will need to be sure to solidify the basics. More on that later! For now, let's discuss some general test taking strategies that you can apply specifically to the math section.

**For starters, spend the time on the questions that are most likely to award you points.** Each question is worth the same number of points, so you want to dedicate your time to the questions that are suited to your strengths first. The questions on this section get progressively harder, so you don't want to rush through the first half in an attempt to get to the final ones, when it's possible those last 10–15 questions won't go your way.

The best way to deal with that last batch of problems will vary from student to student. If you're a very strong math student and want to score at or above a 30 on the math section, you will need to give yourself time to attempt the final problems comfortably. **If math is not your strong suit and you're just looking to improve your score, then you shouldn't worry too much about those final questions.** It's more important that you work diligently through the earlier questions so that you are not misreading or making careless mistakes.

That being said, **there are questions towards the end that you can probably do!** Not all of those questions require deep understanding or even much actual math. They could be testing a lesser-known rule, identity, or definition, which you may know. Regardless of your math skills, you will want to identify those questions and start with the ones that are within your comfort zone (and the ones you can do quickly).

You don't need to master all of the difficult topics to do well on this section, but you should definitely **make sure you solidify your basics.** That's a common mistake that students will make when studying: they won't review the simpler topics. The ACT tests pre-algebra concepts pretty heavily, so you need to refresh your memory on the concepts that you may have learned before you even got to high school. Something as simple as what a prime number is. Don't neglect these things.

..............................................................................................................................

Let's talk about how to avoid some common mistakes on the actual exam.

**Use your calculator wisely.** The calculator is a blessing and a curse: if you're not careful it can lead you in the wrong direction. You don't want to trust it implicitly; you should always be mentally checking to see if what it's spitting out makes sense. This is especially important with negative numbers and exponents. Some calculator tips to avoid these mishaps:

- Input things one step at a time and avoid one long string of text
- Use parentheses when dealing with negatives and exponents
- Double check to make sure you are in the correct mode (usually degree, not radian)

While we're on the topic of calculators, remember that you can OBSERVE a lot of things with the graphing function. Any questions dealing with the behavior of a function or graph –minimums/maximums, intercepts, zeros, points of intersections with other graphs, asymptotes, and points of discontinuity – can be answered by graphing and observing.

You can use the graphing component of your calculator to solve annoying equations. If you have a really ugly equation you don't want to solve by hand, put one side of the formula into one y= and the other side of the formula into another y=, graph it, and find where the two graphs intersect. We'll review this a bit more later.

Back to our strategies. **Make sure you double check what the question is asking for.** You can even circle the question itself if you need to. Very often, you may solve an equation properly, but lose points because you ignore what they're actually looking for. This is especially problematic for equations with more than one variable and geometry problems where you might have a lot of elements going on at once. If they ask for the width, make sure you give them the width and not the length, or vice versa. **Get in the habit of rereading the last line of the question AFTER you've completed your calculations.** It's easy to forget what it was you were solving for, so give yourself a reminder. Don't default to solving an equation, circling that choice, and moving on.

Also be sure to **keep track of your variables** and know what they represent. You don't always have to use "x" and "y." If a word problem has to do with bracelets and necklaces, use "b" to represent bracelets and "n" to represent necklaces. It's easier to keep track of what your variables mean this way.

**Circle key words/phrases in the question.** This will help you break up some of the wordier problems by visually indicating to you what's important, but it will also keep you from ignoring some of the specific requirements they laid out for you. Terms like odd/even, positive/negative, rational/irrational, smallest/largest, prime, integer, two-digit are all really important characteristics that will change the scope of the problem.

Also, **look out for any capitalized or italicized language**, especially when units of measurement are involved. The italics are probably indicating there's a mixture of units. If they give you a unit conversion at the end of the problem, that's also a pretty big sign that you need to be mindful of the units in the problem and do some converting.

Keep an eye out for one of the biggest pitfalls of all: mishandling negatives. Careless mistakes are bound to happen, but if you deal with signed numbers carefully, that will go a long way. The ACT will always predict the most common careless errors students will make and give you answer choices that line up with those missteps, so you have to be detail-oriented even on the simplest of problems. **Pay attention to the order of operations and be very careful with negatives.** If careless mistakes are an ongoing issue, be sure to check your answers after solving. Plug it back into the original equation if there is one, and see if it works out. It may seem like a time waster, but ultimately, you'll only be using up a few seconds and you can catch mistakes easily this way.

........................................................................................................................................

Let's take a bit of time to talk about what to do in the event that you don't know how to get started with a problem. That's a common issue, because you might be familiar with the relevant topics and formulas, but the material could be presented to you in a way that you've never seen before. When you don't have a procedure in mind, you have to ask yourself some prompting questions to get the ball rolling. That will get easier the more you practice.

**Start by writing down a formula when you can (see formula sheet).** If you can figure out which concept is being tested, write out the formulas you know regarding that topic. The average/mean formula, for example, is a commonly tested one. After you've written down the formula, you can go back into the text and determine what they've given you directly (or indirectly) and plug those values into the formula. You may need to revisit the formula more than once or use multiple formulas, but your job will mostly be figuring out what's been given, what can be determined with a little work, and ultimately what you're solving for.

Certain formulas you don't really think to write out. You may default to doing an operation right away. Mistakes can easily happen this way. You might divide instead of multiplying when you're trying to do something theoretically vs. actually writing out the steps. Theoretical operations also won't help for trickier problems where there are variables involved and not everything is given to you strictly with numbers, so don't underestimate the power of physically writing out the formula.

**Step "outside" the problem.** When things start to feel overwhelming, don't focus on the specifics of the problem. Start by identifying the underlying concept being tested. Once you have the concept, think of a formula or procedure that aligns with that concept. Then step back "in" the problem and determine what you've been given and what you still need. This type of simplification is especially important for grouped questions. Those can be very visually overstimulating if you allow yourself to get distracted by all the information presented to you (a good portion of which may not be relevant or necessary for individual questions).

**When in doubt, just start manipulating an expression or equation any way that you can.** When you don't know exactly how to solve a problem, try to play around with the equation, even if you're not exactly sure why. Think less about what you "should" do and more about what you "could" do. Ask yourself if you can distribute, factor, cross multiply, combine like terms or group similar terms to one side of an equation, expand terms, or use the conjugate. Every time you perform an action, run through the list again until you get to an end result.

Speaking of manipulating, **you may need to tweak your answer** after you solve something correctly. If you're fairly confident you've worked through something correctly, but then look at the answer choices and don't see yours listed, don't panic. If it's algebraic, they may have reworked the expression a bit. If it's numerical, you may have calculated your answer in a different form. You may end up with a decimal only to see answers written as fractions, or radicals, or in terms of pi. You'll simply just need to figure out which of the answer choices matches up to yours by putting the answer choices into the calculator to determine their values.

Keep in mind that answer choices that are close to the one you got but not quite the same are probably wrong. "x-y" looks a whole lot like "y-x" but they are very different things. If they ask for a value "closest to" the answer or ask for an approximation, that's when you can feel free to pick an answer choice that's close numerically. But if that is not specified, or if the choices are algebraic, answers that are similar but still different are likely incorrect.

**Try to eliminate answer choices, even when you don't know how to fully solve a problem.** Process of elimination is something students default to for the other sections, but won't utilize on the math section. It's not as habitual; you may see a problem, think "I don't know how to do that," and move on, but you should always try to eliminate as many choices as possible to give yourself better odds when guessing. You may not know enough to solve entirely, but you might know enough about a topic to eliminate even one or two choices. Try to force yourself not to give up. Focus on what you DO know about a topic and see if that gives you enough information to narrow it down.

........................................................................................................................................

Let's wrap up with a few general tips. **Mark up diagrams or draw your own.** Visualizations (especially with geometry problems) can make all the difference so draw out the scenario or figure if it's not provided for you. If you're given something in the x-y plane, draw out the plane and physically plot the points. If it's a word problem that you can break down and visually represent somehow, do that. It will be easier to absorb than a giant chunk of text.

**Don't be afraid to play around with the figures they provide.** They always give you enough information to solve a problem, but sometimes you have to get creative and fill in some of the visual gaps. For circle problems, sometimes rotating the radius or drawing a new one is helpful. Drawing lines to create new triangles is also a great tool. Even rotating the figures or taking a figure made up of several shapes and redrawing the shapes individually can help a great deal.

**Get comfortable translating word problems into equations.** Modeling equations from words is an important skill. Know that "more/larger than" signifies addition, "less/fewer than" indicates subtraction, "times as great" indicates multiplication, and the word "is" represents an equal sign. We will discuss this in greater detail later.

**Look for patterns and identities.** Most of the time you can work your way around this, but for the purpose of saving time, these can be really helpful. Special triangles, like the 3-4-5 or 5-12-13 triangles, can shave valuable seconds off a problem if you recognize the pattern and don't default to Pythagorean Theorem.

Lastly, **remember that there is often more than one way to solve a problem.** You don't have to solve it the way the ACT wants you to. You can solve things logically, algebraically, or graphically. **You can also backsolve or use test values if you're truly stuck.** On that note, be careful using 0, 1, or 2 as test values, and if you do decide to plug in the answer choices, start with the middlemost value. You may be able to determine if you need a larger number or smaller number based on what you observe.

Above all, manage your time well. There's no time to be stubborn on the ACT, so if a problem is not going your way, skip it and come back to it. The importance of revisiting a problem with fresh eyes can't be stressed enough. Staring at something for too long won't help, but very often when you come back to it later on, something will click, and you won't be chewing up the clock this way. Leave yourself enough time to revisit those questions at the end of the section. Do not waste time on questions that you know how to solve but that will take a substantial amount of time. Some questions are simply time-sucking questions. You need to be wise enough to leave those until last and only attempt them if you have confidently tackled all the other problems. Remember our 5-second rule!

As far as subject matter goes, there is no better way to prepare than to work through several ACT's. As we stated before, each exam is a little different, so it will take working through a substantial amount of tests before you feel like you've been exposed to all of the possible content.

It's not enough to simply familiarize yourself with the relevant formulas/concepts; you need to think about HOW the information is being presented to you on the exam. There is no better way to get up to speed on this than to work through several exams. You'll start to recognize patterns in the way the questions are worded. Make note of these patterns. Determine what key phrases or elements of a question clue you in on what's being tested. Test yourself on that knowledge just as much as you would a formula. Your notes, flashcards, or review sheets should contain bits of information like this. Here's an example:

> Q: "When a question gives me 3 values and asks for a fourth…."

> A: "I'll probably need to set up a proportion"

Before you start to tackle all of the possible topics and questions, **you must first make sure you have mastered your basics.** After all, you have to walk before you can run! Fundamentals are crucial for two reasons. For starters, the first 20–25 questions on the math section will be focused more heavily on these foundational skills, but the later, more complex questions will also require knowledge of these concepts. Math is a subject that inherently builds on itself, so it's nearly impossible to master the challenging material without giving yourself a solid foundation.

That is what we are going to take some time to do now. We will:

- Review definitions and properties of numbers
- Review basic operations: plugging in (and function notation), isolating/solving for a variable, modeling equations, factoring
- Describe some core concepts: probability, proportions, angle properties, percents, properties of lines, and rules for exponents
- List some basic formulas

........................................................................................................

## DEFINITIONS AND PROPERTIES OF NUMBERS

**Integers** are positive and negative whole numbers (so no fractions or decimals). Zero is also considered an integer.

**Rational numbers** are all numbers that can be written as a fraction. This includes fractions (obviously), whole numbers, finite decimals, and repeating decimals. A decimal like .3333333, for example, is the same thing as ⅓ , so it is considered rational. Essentially, rational numbers are the "pretty" numbers.

**Irrational numbers** are numbers that can't be put into fraction form. They are very often radicals. The square root of 2, for example, is irrational. If you put it into your calculator, you will get a long, ugly, non-repeating decimal. Basically, irrational numbers are the "ugly" numbers.

**Prime numbers** are numbers that are only divisible by themselves and 1. Examples of primes are 2, 3, 5, 7, 11, 13, etc. Keep in mind that 2 is the only even prime number.

**Multiples** of a number are all numbers divisible by that number. 16 is a multiple of 4 because 16/4 = 4 and not some decimal.

**Factors** of a number are all the numbers that divide evenly into that number. 5 is a factor of 40 because 40/5 = 8.

**Prime Factorization** is the breakdown of a number into all its prime factors. For example, 24 has a prime factorization of $24 = 2 \cdot 2 \cdot 2 \cdot 3$.

...............................................................................................................................................

### Properties/Behavior of Basic Operations

| | |
|---|---|
| Even + Even = Even | 2 + 2 = 4 |
| Odd + Odd = Even | 3 + 3 = 6 |
| Odd + Even = Odd | 3 + 2 = 5 |
| | |
| Even x Even = Even | 2 x 2 = 4 |
| Odd x Odd = Odd | 3 x 3 = 9 |
| Even x Odd = Even | 2 x 3 = 6 |
| | |
| Positive x Positive = Positive | 2 x 2 = 4 |
| Negative x Negative = Positive | (-2) x (-2) = 4 |
| Negative x Positive = Negative | (-2) x 2 = -4 |
| Positive/ Negative = Negative | 4 / (-2) = -2 |

A negative number raised to an EVEN exponent will give a POSITIVE result.

$$(-2)^2 = 4$$

A negative number raised to an ODD exponent will give a NEGATIVE result.

$$(-2)^3 = -8$$

When you subtract a negative number, that is the same thing as ADDING that number.

$5 - (-3) = 5 + 3 = 8$

## SIMPLE SOLVING/ ISOLATING A VARIABLE

Solving for a single variable is an important skill, so if it is something you struggle with, make sure to practice this a lot. Not only will you have purely algebraic problems that require you to solve in this way, it's also the last step for a lot of the word problems or modeling problems you'll run into.

Remember that when you're getting a variable alone, you're essentially "undoing" anything that's been done to it by performing the "opposite" operation.

- **Addition** is the opposite of **subtraction**
- **Multiplication** is the opposite of **division**
- Taking a **square root** is the opposite of **squaring**

You'll want to "undo" these operations one step at a time in the **opposite** order of PEMDAS. (Although, there are always exceptions to this rule – more on that later!)

So if we have something like:

$$\frac{2}{3}x^2 + 6 = 12$$

We'd start by undoing the addition of 6 by subtracting 6 from each side.

$$\frac{2}{3}x^2 = 6$$

Then we would undo the multiplication of ⅔ by dividing by ⅔. **This is the same thing as multiplying by the reciprocal**– in this case, $\frac{3}{2}$

$$\left(\frac{3}{2}\right)\frac{2}{3}x^2 = 6\left(\frac{3}{2}\right) \quad \Rightarrow \quad x^2 = 9$$

Then we would undo the square by taking the square root of both sides. **When solving for a variable, don't forget to consider both the positive and negative square roots.**

$$\sqrt{x^2} = \sqrt{9} \quad \Rightarrow \quad x = \pm\, 3$$

Now we can't assume that every addition/subtraction can be eliminated first. Things get a bit trickier when the expressions get more involved, but the idea is simple enough: deal with the "bigger" problems first. If something is being done to the *entire* expression, that's the first thing to tackle. The first step does NOT always involve addition/subtraction.

Here's an example:

$$\frac{2x^2 + 6}{3} = 12$$

This equation looks almost identical to the first one we went over, but it is a very different problem. We can't just subtract the 6 from the start. The division by 3 is the "bigger" problem. It's not just the x term being divided by 3 – it's the entire left side of the equation, so we have to address this first.

We would start by multiplying both sides of the equation by 3.

$$2x^2 + 6 = 36$$

Now that we've dealt with the only "bigger" issue, we're free to solve for x normally. Use the following process:

1) Subtract the 6
2) Divide by 2
3) Take the square root

One more example:

$$\sqrt{2x + 10} = (4)$$

We would begin by squaring both sides (as the square root is the "biggest" problem):

$$(\sqrt{2x + 10})^2 = (4)^2$$
$$2x + 10 = 16$$

Then, we subtract 10 from both sides:

2x = 6

And finally divide each side by 2:

x = 3

**Note**: Inequalities containing variables will be dealt with the same way a standard equation is dealt with. The only major difference is that multiplying or dividing by a negative will change the direction of the inequality. Otherwise, the process for isolating the variable is the same!

........................................................................................................................................

**Isolating a variable will not always result in a numerical answer.** Sometimes you'll just end up shifting things in the original equation around so that the variable you care about is alone on one side of the equation. You won't necessarily be working strictly with numbers, but the **same rules apply.** You'll want to undo any operations being performed on that variable.

Conceptually, it probably makes more sense to subtract 3 from something than it does to subtract "y" from something. But that "y" is just a placeholder for a number, so you will work with variables the exact same way you work with numbers. Recall that **you can only combine like terms**. For example:

- Numbers can be combined with other numbers
- $x$ terms can be combined with other $x$ terms
- $x^2$ terms can be combined with other $x^2$ terms

You can only combine variables of the **same name and degree** (have the same exponent). Anything else just doesn't make sense!

- $x$ terms **CANNOT** be combine with $x^2$ terms
- Variables **CANNOT** be combined with numbers

Let's work through an example:

$$\frac{g^2 + B}{4} = M$$

Suppose the question asked us to "solve for g" or to "get g in terms of D and M." Both of these phrases mean the same thing: to get g alone on one side of the equation.

We will work through this the same way we did our earlier examples. We will deal with the 4 first by multiplying both sides of the equation by 4.

$$g^2 + B = 4M$$

Now we can't really multiply the 4 by M to get an actual value; we can only leave it as 4 x M (or 4M). Next, we would deal with the B by subtracting it from both sides of the equation.

$$g^2 = 4M - B$$

We can't actually subtract B from 4M. We can only write it as "4M-B." Our last step is then to take the square root of both sides.

$$g = \sqrt{4M - B}$$

It's not quite as satisfying as ending up with a tangible number, but your job is done!

........................................................................................................................................................

## PLUGGING IN

Plugging in is a simple concept, but that doesn't mean you should rush through it. (After all, sometimes the easiest things are the easiest to mess up.) Several problems on the exam will ask that you simply plug certain values into an expression, but that's not the only way we can use plugging in to our benefit. **It's also a great way to "check" our answers** after we've solved for a variable. Remember, this is especially important if you find that you make a lot of careless mistakes with your calculations. Checking your answer choices by plugging them back in can help you identify an error in your calculations.

Plugging in can also **provide us with a back-up plan when we don't know how to solve something algebraically.** You might remember from our strategies that there is often more than one way to solve a problem. Backsolving (sometimes referred to as PITA: plug in the answers) is an effective strategy to utilize when you don't know how to solve algebraically or think the algebraic approach is too long/complicated.

As far as the actual process goes, plugging in essentially just means that you're **replacing a variable with an actual value** (usually a number – in more complex cases, another variable/expression). When it's purely numbers you're dealing with, this can be done pretty easily with your calculator. Just be sure that you input the values carefully and make good use of parentheses (especially when negatives and exponents are involved).

........................................................................................................................................................

The concept of plugging in goes hand in hand with **function notation**. You've probably seen f(x), g(x), or some variation of this before. F(x) is usually read as "f of x," which means we have some function, f, whose values are determined by inputting different values for x. It doesn't matter if it's a number, another variable, or even an entire expression. The procedure is the same: **replace x with whatever appears inside the parentheses**. Don't get spooked by questions involving function notation just because they look tricky. It usually ends up being pretty basic algebra.

F(3) would simply be whatever value we get after plugging in 3. Remember, "plugging in" just means replacing, so replace x with 3 anywhere it appears in the function.

Here's an example:

$$f(x) = \frac{x^2 - 3x}{4}$$

What is $f(-3)$?

By simply replacing x with -3 in the expression, we'll end up with our answer. Remember to use parentheses carefully if inputting in the calculator.

$$f(-3) = \frac{(-3)^2 - 3(-3)}{4} \quad \Rightarrow \quad \frac{18}{4}$$

---

When there are two functions defined, sometimes you will be asked to calculate a composite function, which is when one function gets substituted into the other. There are two major notations for this:

1) $f(g(x))$
2) $f \circ g(x)$

Both are read as "f of g of x." You will probably see the first notation more often. The important thing to remember is to **start with the "inner" function** or the function that appears **closer to the variable**. The same idea applies: you will replace the variables with whatever value or expression appears in the parentheses. Let's work through an example:

$$f(x) = 5x - 1 \qquad g(x) = x^2 + 3$$

To calculate $f(g(x))$, we would replace x with $g(x)$ wherever x appears in $f$.

$$f(g(x)) = 5(x^2 + 3) - 1$$

We can then clean things up by distributing and combining like terms. Let's take it one step further and input a value for x.

$$f(g(5)) = 5((5)^2 + 3) - 1$$

**Note:** *fg*(x) is NOT the same as a composite function. If the "o " symbol is missing, this means the functions are being multiplied by each other, not composed.

.................................................................................................................................................

## FACTORING

Factoring is a helpful tool for rewriting expressions or determining the zeros of a polynomial. Zeros, roots, solutions, and x-intercepts all mean the same thing: whatever x values will make the function equal to 0. There are three basic types of factoring we will review:

1) Factoring a trinomial (usually a quadratic)
2) Pulling out a GCF
3) Difference of two squares

.................................................................................................................................................

### TRINOMIALS

A trinomial is a polynomial with three terms, very often quadratics with a front term (usually x) that is squared.

The standard form of a quadratic is:

$$ax^2 + bx + c$$

To factor a quadratic whose leading coefficient (a) is equal to 1, you must find two integers that multiply to c and add to b. It's a way of anticipating what would happen if you used FOIL to go back from the factored form of the quadratic to the original equation.

Ex: $x^2 + 5x + 4$

Two numbers that multiply to 4 and add to 5 are 4 and 1, so in factored form, this trinomial will look like:

$$(x+4)(x+1)$$

To calculate the zeros (sometimes called solutions) of a polynomial, bring all terms to one side of an equation and factor. Then take each factor, set it equal to 0, and solve for x. This works because if either of the terms in the parentheses can be made to equal zero, then the whole expression will equal zero.

$$(x+4)(x+1) = 0$$

$$
\begin{array}{cc}
x+4=0 & x+1=0 \\
\underline{-4 \quad -4} & \underline{-1 \quad -1} \\
x=-4 & x=-1
\end{array}
$$

If all of the terms are not on one side of an equation, you must first move everything to one side and combine like terms before factoring.

$$
\begin{array}{c}
x^2 + x - 8 = 3x - 7 \\
\underline{-3x \ +7 \quad -3x \ +7} \\
x^2 - 2x - 1 = 0
\end{array}
$$

If you cannot find two integers that will multiply to c and add to b, you must use the quadratic formula to find the roots:

$$\frac{-b \pm \sqrt{b^2 - 4ac}}{2a}$$

The quadratic formula will work for any quadratic, not just the ones that won't factor easily by hand. Quadratics with leading coefficients not equal to 1 are good examples of quadratics best solved with the quadratic formula.

---

## FACTORING WITH A GCF

Sometimes the only way to factor is with a greatest common factor (GCF). The GCF is a number/term that all of your original terms are multiples of. You will "pull out" that term in front and leave what is "left over" of each original term in a set of parentheses. When we "pull out" a term, we are dividing.

To determine the GCF, look first for a number that divides into all of the terms' coefficients. Then see if there are any variables in common. You can pull out the term with the lowest degree (exponent).

Here's an example:

$$4x^5 - 16x^2$$

The two terms both have a numerical factor of 4. They also share an x variable. The lowest degree of either term is 2, so we can pull out an x2.

$$4x^2\left(x^3 - 4\right)$$

GCF

What's left over when we divided the first term by the GCF

What's left over when we divided the second term by the GCF

**Note:** When we divide terms with exponents, we **subtract** exponents

**Note:** If a term is completely divisible by the GCF, **it does not disappear**. We need to put a "1" in its place.

---

## DIFFERENCE OF TWO SQUARES

A difference of two squares, as the name suggests, is a two-term polynomial where one term is being subtracted from the other. These are typically both perfect square terms (meaning they have whole number square roots).

To factor:

1) Draw two sets of parentheses.

2) Place the square root of the first term at the front of each set of parentheses.

3) Place the square root of the second term at the back of each set of parentheses.

4) Put an addition sign in one set of parentheses and a subtraction sign in the other.

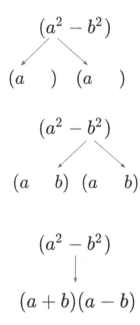

No matter what the method of factoring, to determine a polynomial's roots/zeros, simply take each factor, set it equal to zero, and solve for $x$. **All polynomials are divisible by** $(x - k)$ **if** $k$ **is a root.**

................................................................................................................

## MODELING

Modeling is essentially a process of building equations or expressions from a word problem. Sometimes you will then have to solve for the variable (or variables), but sometimes you'll just be asked to model the equation!

Get familiar with the most common language.

- **"Is"** translates to an equal sign.

- **"More than, larger than, longer than,"** and **"sum"** translate to addition.

- **"Less than, smaller than, shorter than,"** and **"difference"** translate to subtraction

- **"Times as much"** and **"product"** translate to multiplication

Also look for words like "per," "each," and "every." These typically mean that multiplication by a variable is necessary. If there's some numerical <u>value</u> (whether it be cost, price, weight, volume) associated with a variable, you will **multiply** that value by the variable to determine a <u>total</u> cost/price/weight/volume.

For example, if a worker earns 15 dollars *per* hour, the **total earnings** would be found by taking that individual value (15) and multiplying by the number of hours. If the number of hours is unknown, we use a variable in its place. You will see later in this chapter that the total cost formula is one of the basic formulas emphasized. It goes hand in hand with modeling problems.

.......................................................................................................................................

## PROBABILITY

Probability is the likelihood that an event will occur. Questions involving probability are typically very straightforward; you simply need to be detail-oriented. It's very likely you'll see more than one on any given test, so it's a good, simple topic to nail down.

The key idea is that probability is written as a fraction where the number of **total possible outcomes** is your denominator and the number of **desired outcomes** is your numerator.

$$Probability = \frac{desired\ outcomes}{total\ outcomes}$$

So, if there is a bowl containing 20 marbles and 8 of them are red, the probability of selecting a red marble is:

$$\frac{\#\ of\ red\ marbles}{\#\ of\ total\ marbles} = \frac{8}{20}$$

Some of the slightly fancier problems may ask you about the probability that more than one event occurs. In this case you will have to combine individual probabilities according to the wording of the question and the rules below. Read carefully.

- If it's an **"or"** statement (and there's no overlap between the two events), you **add** the individual probabilities. Ex. "What's the probability of having blue eyes **OR** being 6ft tall?" This can be broken down to two events: 1) Odds of having blue eyes and 2) odds of being 6ft tall. Because these are independent probabilities, the individual odds can just be added to get an answer.

- If it's an **"and"** or **"both"** statement, you **multiply** the individual probabilities. Ex. "What's the probability of having blue eyes AND being 6ft tall?" This can be broken down to two events as in the previous example. However, as the question is phrased as **"AND"** the individual odds will be multiplied to get the answer.

......................................................................................................................

### PROPORTIONS

Proportions are used to determine a missing value in a relationship. When we are given one *complete* relationship between two variables and one *incomplete* relationship between two variables of the same kind, we will set up a portion. Keep in mind, proportions are always related to one another through some sort of **scale factor**, which is basically fancy language for multiplication. One relationship is always being multiplied or divided by something to give us the second relationship.

Proportions can pop up in a number of scenarios. They can be part of a word problem (recipes and surveys are common) or part of a geometry problem (like questions involving similar triangles or scale drawings). They can be used to convert units, and they can even pop up in trigonometry. The important thing is identifying when to use them, and **setting them up carefully.** There's always more than one way to set up a proportion, but we do want to make sure whatever way we choose, we are keeping things **consistent and properly lined up.**

This is a concept more easily understood through example.

If a recipe calls for 2 eggs and 5 cups of flour, but you want to alter the recipe to use 3 eggs, how many cups of flour would you need?

Let's start with the relationship we know. We know for certain that 2 eggs will be paired with 5 cups of flour. We'll use that to set up the left side of the equation.

$$\frac{2}{5} = \frac{?}{?}$$

To properly set up the right side, we need to make sure we maintain the pattern on the left side. We placed the number of eggs on top, and the cups of flour on the bottom, so we will do the same on the right side. We already know that 3 eggs will be used, so we will place the 3 in the **numerator** of the right fraction. Since we don't know how many cups of flours we need, we will put an $x$ in the **denominator**.

$$\frac{2\ eggs}{5\ cups} = \frac{3\ eggs}{x\ cups}$$

Once the proportion is properly set up, all you have to do is cross multiply and solve for $x$.

............................................................................................................

## PERCENTS

Percents are used **to indicate portions of a whole.** You will see them frequently in word problems dealing with tax or discounts. Regardless of the specifics of the problem, the first thing you want to do is **change the percent into decimal form** so that it can be used to perform actual calculations.

To do that, we simply take the decimal and move it two spaces **to the left**. You have to be careful and make sure you move it the **full** two spaces and use a zero as a place holder if necessary. For example, 5% is **not** .5. It is .05.

Sometimes it's difficult to figure out which value in a problem should be multiplied by the actual percentage. **Look for the word "of" to help you.** Whatever you're taking the percentage **OF** is what gets multiplied by the percent. Sometimes that will be an unknown value, so we'll multiply the percentage by a variable. If a question reads "30 is 10% of what number," I can't just multiply .10 by 30. I want 10% **OF** some unknown value, so the percent (.10) will be multiplied by a variable. The equation would read: .1$x$ = 30

If the percent is part of a bigger word problem, more work may be involved. The procedure after you've calculated the percentage will come down to the specifics of the problem and you'll have to use your judgement to arrange the equation correctly. If it's a problem involving tax, you're going to be adding that value to your initial cost. Interest on loans or savings accounts typically indicate growth, so you will add values in these circumstances as well. If it's a discount, you'll be subtracting that value from the initial amount. Decay or any sort of decline will also indicate subtraction.

Word problems like this can very often be dealt with in ONE step by using a simplified version of the exponential growth formula.

$$A = I(1 \pm r)^t$$

In this formula, $I$ represents the initial value, $r$ represents the rate (or percentage) written as a decimal, $t$ represents time, and $A$ represents the final value of the growth. Because problems dealing with tax or sales are only happening once, we can replace t with "1" and ignore it after that.

If an item has an original price of $60 dollars and you receive a discount of 25%, you can use this formula to calculate the final amount ($A$) in one step. The initial price ($I$) is 60. The rate ($r$) is .25. Since it is a discount, we will SUBTRACT the .25 from 1.

$$A = 60 \, ( \, 1 - .25)$$
$$A = 60 \, ( \, .75)$$
$$A = 45$$

......................................................................................................................

## ANGLE PROPERTIES

Properties of angles are simple enough if you can commit them to memory. The four that are the most important are:

1) Angles that lie on a straight line will add up to 180 degrees.

2) Angles in a triangle will add up to 180 degrees.

3) Vertical angles (opposite angles formed by two intersecting lines) are congruent.

4) Alternate interior angles are congruent.

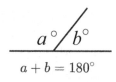

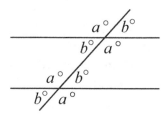

It's also helpful to know **that angles opposite congruent sides in a triangle are also congruent.**

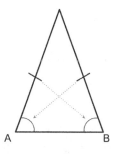

Questions with figures containing missing angles will usually require to use some combination of these rules. Just fill in the figure one angle measure at a time with these guidelines until you arrive at the angle in question.

......................................................................................................................

## PROPERTIES OF LINES

Lines are used to represent **steady** change from a fixed starting point. For each bit you run, you rise the same amount. While the equation of a line can be presented to you in many ways, a very useful lens through which to view it is the standard form below

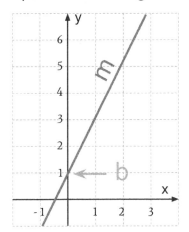

**Equation of a Line**

$$y = mx + b$$

**Slope (m)** is how quickly the line is changing. A large value of "m" makes a line steep; a small value makes it shallow. The formula for slope has a few different variations, the most common being:

$$m = \frac{y_1 - y_2}{x_1 - x_2}$$

This version is most helpful when given two points. **Note:** It does not matter which point you choose for "$y_2$," as long as you make sure to match it with "$x_2$."

Slope is also very often referred to as:

$$\frac{rise}{run} \quad \text{or} \quad \frac{change\ in\ y}{change\ in\ x}$$

**Note:** Not all linear equations will use the variables "x" and "y"; those are simply the variables we are most familiar with. If you are given an equation with different variables, determine which variable is acting as your "y" and which one is acting as your "x." The "y," which is your **dependent variable**, is typically alone on one side of the equation.

................................................................

**The y intercept** is the point on the y-axis where the line crosses over. This is the "$b$" term in our standard equation.

When asked about the slope or y-intercept of a line, it is crucial that you **first isolate y**. Once you have the equation in standard form, those values are **clearly presented** as constants in the equation.

................................................................

Lastly, you should know how parallel lines and perpendicular lines relate to one another algebraically.

- The slopes of **parallel** lines are **equal**
- The slope of **perpendicular** lines are **negative reciprocals** of one another.

## MATRIX BASICS

Matrices will not account for too many questions on the exam, but certain matrix operations are very simple to nail down. That makes it a great topic to become familiar with. Any matrix problems found in the earlier questions will likely require you to do one of two things: add matrices together or multiply a matrix by a scale factor.

A **matrix** is a rectangular collection of numbers. Matrices are defined by their dimensions: (the number of rows) x (the number of columns).

This is a 2 x 3 matrix (2 rows and 3 columns):

$$\begin{pmatrix} 6 & 2 & 7 \\ 4 & -1 & 0 \end{pmatrix}$$

## ADDITION/SUBTRACTION

You can add/subtract two (or more) matrices together **if they are the same size.** You simply add/subtract the values in the corresponding positions (or "spots") in each matrix.

$$\begin{bmatrix} 6 & 2 & 7 \\ 4 & -1 & 0 \end{bmatrix} + \begin{bmatrix} 2 & 3 & -1 \\ 0 & 5 & 6 \end{bmatrix} = \begin{bmatrix} 8 & 5 & 6 \\ 4 & 6 & 6 \end{bmatrix}$$

## SCALAR MULTIPLICATION

You can multiply a matrix by a scalar (outside term) by simply multiplying each entry inside the matrix by that number/term. It's essentially the same thing as distributing.

$$5 \begin{bmatrix} 6 & 2 & 7 \\ 4 & -1 & 0 \end{bmatrix} = \begin{bmatrix} 30 & 10 & 35 \\ 20 & -5 & 0 \end{bmatrix}$$

# BASIC FORMULAS

$$Average = \frac{Sum}{Number\ of\ Terms}$$

...................................................................................................................................

*Total cost (Weight/Price/volume) = Individual cost × number of units*

...................................................................................................................................

$$Velocity = \frac{Distance}{time}$$

**Note:** Be sure units are consistent. If speed is given in miles per hour, the distance must be in miles and the time in hours.

...................................................................................................................................

The **Pythagorean Theorem** relates the lengths of the sides of a right triangle, for the triangle below, it would be:

$$a^2 + b^2 = c^2$$

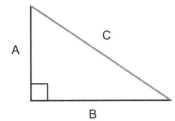

It is important to note here that the "c" term in this formula is the hypotenuse, the longest side, of the triangle. While the "a" and "b" terms are interchangeable, the "c" term is not. When you plug in, be sure to put the longest side there.

...................................................................................................................................

To find the **Midpoint** between two points, $P_1 = (X_1, Y_1)$ and $P_2 = (X_2, Y_2)$, you just take the average of the X and Y values for each point:

$$Midpoint = (X_M, Y_M) = \left(\frac{X_1+X_2}{2}, \frac{Y_1+Y_2}{2}\right)$$

...................................................................................................................................

To find the **Distance** between two points, $P_1 = (X_1, Y_1)$ and $P_2 = (X_2, Y_2)$, you just find the difference of the X and Y values for each point and plug those into the Pythagorean Theorem:

$$Distance = d = \sqrt{(x_1 - x_2)^2 + (y_1 - y_2)^2}$$

.............................................................................................................................

The formulas for the **perimeter** and **area** of common geometric figures can be found in the table below.

While there is a more complete formula sheet at the end of this section (which will also include basic **volume** formulas), these are the ones that you ought to have committed to memory by exam day. If you can recall these quickly, it will go a long way towards helping you ace the first 30 questions.

| Name of Figure | Perimeter | Area/Surface Area |
|---|---|---|
| Triangle | a+b+c | $(1/2)\, bh$ |
| Circle | $2\pi r$ | $\pi r^2$ |
| Rectangle | $2w + 2l$ | $w \cdot l$ |
| Square | $4s$ | $s^2$ |

.............................................................................................................................

## RULES FOR EXPONENTS

You will see a more detailed collection of rules for exponents on the formula sheet, but the following are the most commonly tested and the most crucial to remember.

$$a^x a^y = a^{x+y} \qquad\qquad \frac{a^x}{a^y} = a^{x-y}$$

$$\left(a^x\right)^y = a^{xy} \qquad\qquad a^{\frac{x}{y}} = \sqrt[y]{a^x}$$

# FORMULA SHEET

## Properties of Numbers

$$(+) \times (+) = (+)$$
$$(-) \times (-) = (+)$$
$$(-) \times (+) = (-)$$
$$(-) \div (+) = (-)$$

Even + Even = Even
Odd + Odd = Even
Odd + Even = Odd

Even x Even = Even
Odd x Odd = Odd
Even x Odd = Even

**Multiples** of a number are all numbers divisible by that number
**Factors** of a number are all the numbers that divide evenly into that number
**Prime Factorization** is the breakdown of a number into all its prime factors

## Basic Formulas/Concepts

$$Distance = speed \times time$$

$$Total\ cost = cost\ per\ unit \times \#\ of\ units$$
(cost/price/weight/volume/area)

$$Average = \frac{Sum}{\#\ of\ terms}$$
(Mean)

The **mode** is the value that appears most often in a set
The **median** is the middlemost value (**after** ordering)

$$Part = Percent(as\ decimal) \times whole$$

$$Percent\ Change = \frac{Ending - Initial}{Initial} \times 100$$

Quadratic Formula: $\dfrac{-b \pm \sqrt{b^2 - 4ac}}{2a}$

When converting:
From larger unit to smaller unit: **multiply**
From smaller unit to larger unit: **divide**

## Properties of Exponents and Radicals

$$a^x a^y = a^{x+y} \qquad a^{\frac{x}{y}} = \sqrt[y]{a^x} \qquad (ab)^n = a^n b^n \qquad a^0 = 1$$

$$\frac{a^x}{a^y} = a^{x-y} \qquad a^{-x} = \frac{1}{a^x} \qquad \sqrt[n]{ab} = \sqrt[n]{a} \times \sqrt[n]{b}$$

$$(a^x)^y = a^{xy} \qquad \frac{1}{a^{-x}} = a^x \qquad \sqrt[n]{\frac{a}{b}} = \frac{\sqrt[n]{a}}{\sqrt[n]{b}}$$

## Geometry Basics

$$A = lw$$
$$P = 2l + 2w$$
Diagonal length: $\sqrt{l^2 + w^2}$

$$V = lwh$$
Diagonal length: $\sqrt{l^2 + w^2 + h^2}$

$$A = \pi r^2$$
$$C = \pi d$$

$$V = \pi r^2 h$$

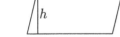

$$A = bh$$

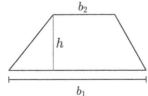

$$A = \frac{1}{2}(b_1 + b_2)h$$

Coordinate Circle Formula:
$$(x - h)^2 + (y - k)^2 = r^2$$
Where (h,k) is the center, r is the radius

$$A = \frac{1}{2}bh$$

Angles **opposite** congruent sides are congruent

Similar triangles have **congruent** angles and **proportional** side lengths

$$\frac{x°}{360°} = \frac{\overset{\frown}{AB}}{circumference}$$

$$\frac{x°}{360°} = \frac{sector\ area}{circle\ area}$$

## Angles and Lines

$$y = mx + b$$

where *m* is slope and *b* is the y-intercept

Slope (m) = $\dfrac{change\ in\ y}{change\ in\ x} = \dfrac{rise}{run} = \dfrac{y_1 - y_2}{x_1 - x_2}$

Midpoint = $\left( \dfrac{x_1 + x_2}{2}, \dfrac{y_1 + y_2}{2} \right)$

Distance = $\sqrt{(x_1 - x_2)^2 + (y_1 - y_2)^2}$

Parallel lines have equal slopes
Perpendicular lines have slopes that are negative reciprocals

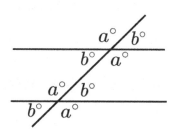

$$a + b = 180°$$

For all polygons with n sides, the sum of the interior angles is $(n-2)180°$

## Probability

Event Probability $= \dfrac{Desired\ Outcomes}{Total\ Outcomes}$

$$P(A \cap B) = P(A) \times P(B)$$

$$P(A \cup B) = P(A) + P(B) - P(A \cap B)$$

## Combinations/Permutations

For combinations (where order does **not** matter):

$$_nC_r = \dfrac{n!}{r!(n-r)!}$$

For permutations (where order **does** matter):

$$_nP_r = \dfrac{n!}{(n-r)!}$$

Where n is the number of options and r is the number of things you are ordering/selecting

## Trigonometry and Triangle Properties

For all right triangles:

$$a^2 + b^2 = c^2$$

Special Right Triangles:
3 - 4 - 5
5 - 12 - 13
*and multiples of each

$$sin(x) = \dfrac{Opposite}{Hypotenuse}$$

$$cos(x) = \dfrac{Adjacent}{Hypotenuse}$$

$$tan(x) = \dfrac{Opposite}{Adjacent}$$

$$sin^2(x) + cos^2(x) = 1$$

For all non-right triangles:

\* $c^2 = a^2 + b^2 - 2ab\,cos(C)$

\* $\dfrac{Sin(A)}{a} = \dfrac{Sin(B)}{b} = \dfrac{Sin(C)}{c}$

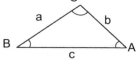

*do not need to memorize

## Additional Topics

For arithmetic sequences (with a common **difference**):

To find the $n^{th}$ term: $a_n = a_1 + d(n-1)$

To find the sum of the first *n* terms: $S_n = \frac{n}{2}(a_1 + a_n)$

For geometric sequences (with a common **ratio**):

To find the $n^{th}$ term: $a_n = a_1 r^{n-1}$

To find the sum of the first *n* terms: $S_n = a_1 \left( \frac{1 - r_n}{1 - r} \right)$

$log_b a = c \rightarrow b^c = a$

$log_b b = 1$

$log_b a^x = x\,log_b a$

$\begin{vmatrix} a & b \\ c & d \end{vmatrix} = ad - bc$

- You can add matrices of the **same** dimension by adding corresponding positions together
- You can multiply a matrix by a scalar by multiplying each position by that scalar
- You can multiply matrices when the **column** dimension of the first equals the **row** dimension of the second: $(m \times n)(n \times p)$

The resulting matrix will have dimensions: $(m \times p)$

# CALCULATOR TIPS AND TRICKS

First thing's first, let's talk about which calculators you are permitted to use. Most of you are using some form of a TI-83 or TI-84, which is perfectly legal. Although a graphing calculator isn't necessary, it is an incredibly useful tool. If you were planning on using a scientific calculator, strongly consider upgrading to a calculator with a graphing component. The TI-84 Plus CE is a great option. Check out curvebreakerstestprep.com for some detailed blog posts discussing calculators.

Below is a list of all of the calculators that are **NOT** permitted for the ACT exam.

- Calculators with built-in or downloaded computer algebra system functionality, including:

**Texas Instruments:**
- All model numbers that begin with TI-89 or TI-92
- TI-Nspire CAS
  *Note: The TI-Nspire (non-CAS) is permitted.*

**Hewlett- Packard:**
- HP Prime
- HP 48GII
- All model numbers that begin with HP 40G, HP 49G, or HP 50G

**Casio:**
- fx-CP400 (ClassPad 400)
- ClassPad 300 or ClassPad 330
- Algebra fx 2.0
- All model numbers that begin with CFX-9970G

- Handheld, tablet, or laptop computers (including PDAs)

- Electronic writing pads or pen-input devices
  *Note: The Sharp EL 9600 is permitted.*

- Calculators built into cell phones or any other electronic communication devices

- Calculators with QWERTY format letter keys
  - This does not apply to calculators that are provided in a secure test delivery platform.
  - Letter keys not in QWERTY format **are** permitted.

Now that that's settled, let's discuss some functions of the calculator.

## Inputting a Fraction

1) Press "alpha"
2) Press "y="
3) 3) Press "enter" to select "1:n/d"

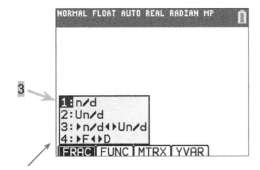

**NOTE:** There are several other function you'll see in this list.
"2: Un/d" will allow you to input a mixed number
"3: ▶n/d ◀ ▶Un/d" will change a fraction into a mixed number

**To get a decimal in fraction form:**

1) Press "math"

2) Press "enter" to select "1: ▶ Frac"

3) Press "enter"

\* To get from fraction form into decimal, repeat the procedure, but select "2: Dec"

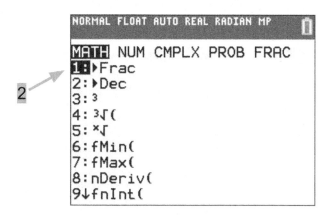

**Logarithm with a Base not equal to 10:**

1) Press "math"

2) Scroll down to "A: LogBASE("

3) Press "enter"

4) Input base and what you are calculating the logarithm of

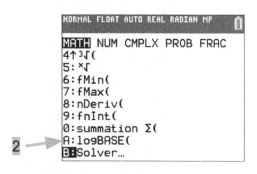

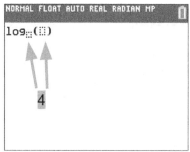

## Scientific Notation

1) Press "mode"

2) Scroll down to second row and select "SCI"

3) Quit (Press 2nd and then "mode" to quit)

## Calculating A Remainder

1) Press "math"

2) Scroll right to "num"

3) Scroll down to "0: remainder( "

4) Press "enter"

5) Input your dividend (what you're dividing)

6) Input a comma

7) Input your divisor (what you're dividing by)

8) Close parenthesis and press "enter"

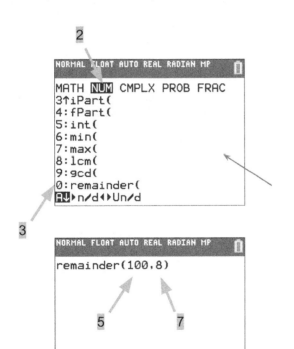

**NOTE:** There are several other functions you'll see in this list that can be calculated with the same steps.

- "8: lcm( " will calculate a least common multiple

- "9: gcd( " will calculate a greatest common divisor

   *Place commas between your terms.

**To find a zero (solution or root) by graphing**

1) Press "y="

2) Input function into Y1=

3) Press "graph" (the graph will appear in your window; if it does not, try zooming out by pressing "zoom" and scrolling down to "3: zoom out" )

4) Press "2ND" and then "trace"

5) Scroll down to "2: zero" and press "enter"

6) Move the cursor to a spot on the curve to the LEFT of the zero. Push "enter"

7) Move the cursor to a spot on the curve to the RIGHT of the zero. Push "enter"

8) Push "enter" a third time

9) The x and y coordinates will appear at the bottom of the screen

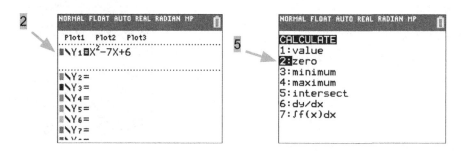

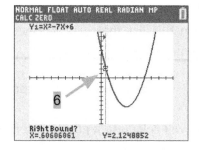

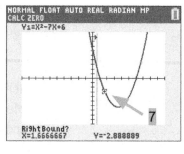

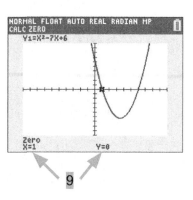

**NOTE:** You can find a maximum or minimum with the same procedure. In step 5, select:

- "3: minimum" to trace a minimum
- "4: maximum" to trace a maximum

## To find a point of intersection

1) Press "y="

2) Input first function into Y1=

3) Input second function into Y2=

4) Press "graph"  (both graphs will appear in your window; if they do not, try zooming out by pressing "zoom" and scrolling down to "3: zoom out")

5) Press "2ND" and then "trace"

6) Scroll down to "5: intersect" and press "enter"

7) Move the cursor to a spot near the intersection on t he FIRST curve. Push "enter"

8) Move the cursor to a spot near the intersection on the SECOND curve. Push "enter"

9) Push "enter" a third time

10) The x and y coordinates will appear at the bottom of the screen

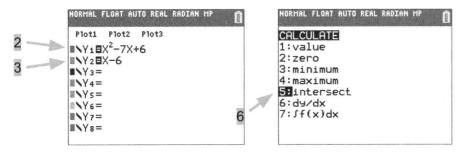

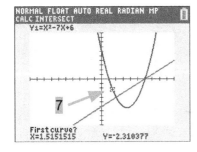

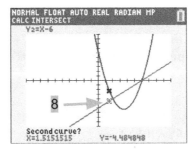

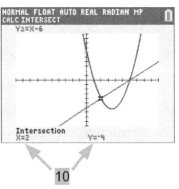

**NOTE**: This is a great way to solve equation that are difficult to solve by hand.

- Put one side of the equation into Y1=
- Put the other side of the equation into Y2=
- Trace the intersection

**NOTE**: A great way to test for **equivalency** (without needing to do the algebra) is to use the graphing component. Put one expression into Y1 and the other expression into Y2 and graph them both. If the functions are truly equivalent, they will have the same graphs.

They will also have the same table values. Viewing the t able might be quicker than letting the calculator graph the entire functions. To locate a table:

1) Press "2nd"

2) Press "graph"

| NORMAL FLOAT AUTO REAL RADIAN MP | | | | |
|---|---|---|---|---|
| PRESS + FOR △Tbl | | | | |
| X | Y1 | Y2 | | |
| 9 | 24 | 3 | | |
| 10 | 36 | 4 | | |
| 11 | 50 | 5 | | |
| 12 | 66 | 6 | | |
| 13 | 84 | 7 | | |
| 14 | 104 | 8 | | |
| 15 | 126 | 9 | | |
| 16 | 150 | 10 | | |
| 17 | 176 | 11 | | |
| 18 | 204 | 12 | | |
| 19 | 234 | 13 | | |

X=9

**NOTE:** The physical graphs, trace functions, and table values can help you determine several features about a function without needing to perform any operations by hand. You can simply *observe* them. These features include:

1) Y- Intercepts and X- Intercepts (zeros)

2) Maximums & Minimums

3) Points of Intersection

4) Points of Discontinuity

5) Asymptotes

6) Limits

7) Equivalencies to other functions

**To determine the factors of a number**

1) Press "y="

2) Input that number divided by x into Y1

3) Press "2ND" and then "graph" to bring you to the table

4) Any x-y pairs that are whole numbers are factors of that initial value

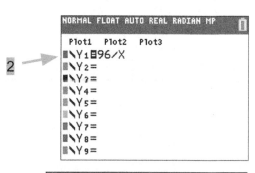

2 →

| NORMAL FLOAT AUTO REAL RADIAN MP | | |
|---|---|---|
| Plot1  Plot2  Plot3 | | |
| ■\Y1⊟96/X | | |
| ■\Y2= | | |
| ■\Y3= | | |
| ■\Y4= | | |
| ■\Y5= | | |
| ■\Y6= | | |
| ■\Y7= | | |
| ■\Y8= | | |
| ■\Y9= | | |

| NORMAL FLOAT AUTO REAL RADIAN MP | | | | |
|---|---|---|---|---|
| PRESS + FOR △Tbl | | | | |
| X | Y1 | | | |
| 0 | ERROR | | | |
| 1 | 96 | | | |
| 2 | 48 | | | |
| 3 | 32 | | | |
| 4 | 24 | | | |
| 5 | 19.2 | | | |
| 6 | 16 | | | |
| 7 | 13.714 | | | |
| 8 | 12 | | | |
| 9 | 10.667 | | | |
| 10 | 9.6 | | | |

X=0

**To find mean, median, and standard deviation for a data set**

1) Press "stat" and select "edit"

2) If it is a single list with no frequency, add the values into list 1 (L1)

3) Press "stat" and scroll right to "CALC" menu

4) Select "1-Var Stats"

5) Make sure "Freqlist" is blank and then push "enter" 3 times

    x = mean (average)

    σx = standard deviation

    med = median

6) If the list *does* have a frequency, enter the frequency of each term into list 2 (L2) and continue with steps 3 and 4

7) Scroll down to "FreqList" and input (L2) by pressing "2nd" and the number "2"

8) Press "enter" twice

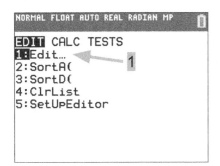

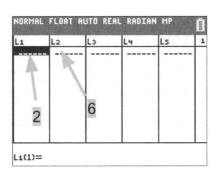

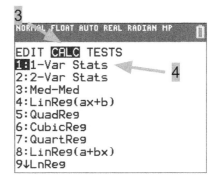

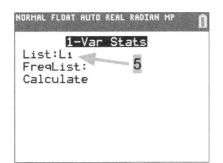

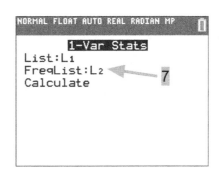

**What you will see**

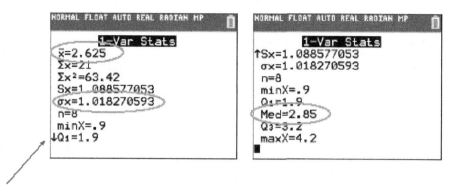

Scroll down to see more information (like the median)

# SUMMARY

- Spend the time on the questions that are most likely to award you points.
- Make sure you solidify your basics.
- Use your calculator wisely.
- Double check what the question is asking.
- Re-read the last line of the question AFTER you've completed your calculations.
- Keep track of your variables.
- Circle key words/phrases in the question.
- Pay attention to the order of operations.
- Be very careful with negatives.
- Start by writing down a formula when you can.
- Step "outside" the problem.
- When in doubt, just start manipulating an expression or equation any way that you can (distribute, factor, combine like terms, cross multiply, etc.).
- You may need to tweak your answer so it matches the available choices.
- Try to eliminate answer choices, even when you don't know how to fully solve a problem.
- Mark up diagrams or draw your own.
- Don't be afraid to play around with the figures they provide.
- Get comfortable translating word problems into equations.
- Look for patterns and identities (like Pythagorean triples).
- Remember that there is often more than one way to solve a problem.
- You can backsolve or use test values if you're truly stuck.

# ACT READING

## WHAT'S THE GIST?

The reading is the third section of the exam. It is made up of 4 passages, each containing 10 multiple choice questions. You will have **35 minutes** to complete **40 questions.**

Each question is a multiple choice question with four possible answer choices.

## WHAT CAN YOU EXPECT TO SEE?

There are four types of passages you can expect to see: literary narrative, social science, humanities, and natural science. While the passages themselves will vary from test to test, the order in which they are presented to you will remain consistent.

You will also be given one "paired passage" containing two smaller excerpts. Any one of the four passages can be presented to you in this manner.

- **Literary Narrative:** Usually consists of excerpts from fiction or literary memoirs

  - Common questions include: main idea/theme, narrator's tone/intent, characterization of relationships/characters, which questions are or are not answered in passage, plot questions

- **Social Science:** Straightforward discussions of topics in the social sciences (psychology, economics, education, sociology, etc.)

  - Common questions include: paraphrasing information found in the passage, determining subject's point of view, which statements the author is likely to agree with

- **Humanities:** Passages can come from personal essays or memoirs, as well as general discussions of humanities subject areas (arts, literature, media, or philosophy, etc.)

  - Common questions include: main idea/theme, narrator's point of view/tone, contrasts between different views/methods mentioned

- **Natural Science:** Nonfictional discussions of natural science topics (biology, physics, astronomy, technology, medicine, etc.)

  - Common questions include: locating specific details, passage layout, relationship between multiple studies/theories

Common questions will include:

- **Main Idea:** Identify main idea of a passage, paragraph, or paragraphs
- **Comparative Relationships:** Interpret similarities and differences between arguments
- **Vocabulary In-Context Questions:** Determine meanings of words in context
- **Sequence of Events:** Determine order of events
- **Author's Voice:** Establish author's mood, tone, and point of view
- **Passage Structure:** Determine layout of passage (recognize shifts in discussion)
- **Details:** Find and interpret details; draw reasonable conclusions from given information

# STRATEGIES

The reading section may take some getting used to because of the time constraints. 35 minutes to do 4 passages is not a lot of time, so you may need to rethink how you're physically reading through these texts. If you try to focus on every word and absorb every detail, you are very likely to run out of time. This section is testing your ability to **quickly** and **efficiently** filter out the **important** information. That's a skill best learned through continued practice, so be prepared to work through a lot of reading passages.

Let's discuss some general strategies before we get into the specifics. First things first, **you want to prioritize the "easier" passages**. "Easy" is going to mean different things to different people. Some of you might find that more scientific, data-driven passages are simpler. Some of you might find that the literary narratives, which are more about picking up on tone and mood, are easier. You'll want to work through a few exams and figure out which passages are best for YOU.

Perhaps even more importantly, you'll want to determine which one is the worst. That's probably the one you should save for last. Like we said earlier, time is a really big factor on this section; even if everything is running smoothly, you'll still probably feel pressed for time on the last passage of the set. You want to make sure this happens on your weakest passage, not your strongest.

You might not find that one passage *type* is any easier than the other. It might come down to the specific topics that are presented to you on any given test. Which brings us to our next strategy: **read the introductory blurbs at the top of each passage.** They will give you an idea of what the passage is about, which might help you decide whether or not you'd like to read through that passage right away. They can also provide you with some great contextual information, like who wrote the passage and when. Perspective can be crucial to your understanding of a passage, *especially* those that are historical in nature.

Passages that contain shorter paragraphs are usually easier and faster to read through. That's something to consider on a test-by-test basis.

**Note:** There is no one-size-fits-all strategy for the reading section. There are several effective ways to order and read through the passages. What works for the majority may not work for you. You might decide to save your strongest/easiest passage for last because it's the one you can tackle confidently in a short time frame. The important thing is always to figure out what works best for you.

......................................................................................................

Let's discuss how to physically read through the passages. In general, you want to **read for the gist**. There are certain parts of a passage that are not important to focus on during the first read-through, like the specific details. You want to walk away from a passage knowing what the main talking points are, what the overall structure and layout of the passage is, and what the author's tone and perspective is when that's applicable.

You can usually get a pretty good sense of all of these things if you **focus on the introduction, the conclusion, and the first and last sentence of each paragraph (I.F.L.C.).** Think about it logically for a moment: the opening and closing statements in a passage or paragraph usually highlight what the main idea is. That's what we care about! The middle portion of a paragraph will mostly contain details, the proof that helps to back up the author's point, but we will only read that *carefully* if and when we're asked about it in the questions. During the first read, we want to know what the <u>overall</u> arguments are and where in the passage those discussions are brought up.

That does not mean we should ignore the information in the other sentences. You'll develop a sense for what information you should pay attention to, and what information is fluff. Transition words – those like "however," "therefore," and "nevertheless"– usually indicate that a <u>significant</u> point is about to be made and that you should pay closer attention to what follows.

After you read one or two paragraphs, **stop to think about what the overall idea was**. If you find it helpful, write down a few words next to those paragraphs that indicate what those paragraphs were about. This can be especially helpful for those moments where we skim through details. Since we are not reading those lines closely, one or two words that indicate what the details are *about* can help us locate information more quickly when we get to the questions.

Keep these mental (or physical) notes simple, but not *too* broad. It's not enough to say to yourself "that paragraph was about crops." Dig a little deeper: What about crops? Is the paragraph about new farming techniques? Is it about the benefits of pesticides? Is it about how certain crops grow better in certain climates? That's the level of takeaway you want to have. Do you need to absorb the fact that squash is best grown in a dense soil in eastward-facing rows? No. Skim over those details quickly.

..................................................................................................................

**Annotate wisely**. The idea of annotating can seem overwhelming at first, but with practice it should become a natural part of taking the exam. For the purpose of the ACT, detailed annotations are not necessary and would chew up too much time. You simply want to use annotations to help you <u>visually pinpoint what's important and create a map of where the details are located</u>.

Determining what's important is where a lot of the anxiety surrounding annotations stems from. That fear is what leads students to frantically underline *everything*, but not everything is important! Even a really important sentence is going to contain a lot of language that's not essential to your understanding. The average sentence is 15–20 words long. That probably sounds absurd, and you're not wrong for thinking that. At the end of the day, there's probably only 4 or 5 words that are really important in the sentence. Focus on that language.

One effective tactic for marking up the passages is what we like to call the circle technique. The goal is to circle the important words in each sentence: the whos, whats, wheres, whens, whys, and hows. The benefit to this type of strategy is threefold: 1) it will help you read more quickly, as your eye will be more inclined to skim over filler words and look for the important terms, 2) the act of circling will help you to absorb the main ideas and identify patterns, and 3) it will provide you visual clues for what individual paragraphs – and by extension, the entire passage – is about. If you're asked about the main purpose of a paragraph, you won't need to reread that paragraph. All of the important language will be circled for you.

Regardless of the strategy you use, the important thing is to not over-do it. Again, the goal is to walk away from the passage with the main talking points and give yourself a map of where the information is located. Think of your circles, notes, and underlines as the basis for a dictionary. When you get to a question that asks you about a specific detail, you're going to need to "look up" that information in the passage. You should be marking the passages in a way that makes this process easier for YOU, however that may look.

Some helpful things to mark up based on the passage type:

- For science- based passages, <u>numbers, names of scientists, names of studies, and important terms that are defined for you</u> may be important things to circle. If you read through a passage that gives you several numerical values, it's likely that you're going to be asked about at least one. Circling them will draw your eye right back to those values

- For the fiction passage, make note of any <u>shifts in perspective or shifts in timeline.</u> If they provide you with some sort of flash-back or memory, it's very likely they will ask you a question about what event occurs first chronologically.

- For fiction passages or any passages where the author's tone is important, circle <u>feeling words.</u> Make note of language that gives you a clue about how the characters feel, even if it's not straightforward. The passage might not say directly that someone was disinterested, but it may say that they slumped in their chair and stared blankly at the clock. Those elements of body language or dialogue with other characters can really help you <u>characterize the people and relationships </u>in the story.

- For all passages, mark up any effective literary devices or quotes. Major shifts in discussion are also important things to make note of.

How to mark up those important items will come down to what you decide is most effective for you. Select a strategy that is not too overwhelming or time consuming. You could:

- Circle or double underline *really* crucial conclusions (or anything that you want the eye to catch like dates, numbers, or names), and underline the more general (but still important) talking points

- Star those shifts in timeline, perspective, or discussion that we were discussing earlier. Or place stars next to full sentences or paragraphs that you think are super important

- Take brief notes next to each paragraph to keep yourself focused and to indicate where the details are located

Again, one of the most important things to keep in mind is that you must work through this section quickly. If you don't absorb every bit of the passage, don't default to rereading (or panicking)! Trust that you can still perform well with the questions even if you only have a loose understanding of the actual text. Also know that **the questions can actually help to build your understanding of the passage if you tackle them wisely**, which is exactly what we'll be discussing next.

Before we do, let's take a look at an example of a marked up excerpt. You'll notice the notes are incredibly brief and that the markings are there strictly to emphasize the key words and patterns (and not to interpret the text).

We live in an age of visual information. Infographics flood the web, driven by accessible platforms that instantly translate information into a variety of graphic forms. News outlets routinely *examples* harvest large data sets like the census and election returns into maps and graphs that profile everything from consumer preferences to the political landscape. The current proliferation of visual information mirrors a similar moment in the early nineteenth century, when the advent of new printing techniques *shift* coincided with the rapid expansion of education. Schoolrooms from the Atlantic seaboard to the Mississippi frontier made room for the children of farmers as well as merchants, girls as well as boys. Together, these shifts created a robust and highly competitive market for school materials, including illustrated textbooks, school atlases, and even the new genre of wall maps.

No individual exploited this publishing opportunity more than Emma Willard, one of the century's most influential educators. From the 1820s through the Civil War, Willard's history and geography textbooks exposed an entire generation of students to her deeply patriotic narratives, all of which were studded with innovative and creative pictures of information that sought to translate big data into manageable visual forms.

Willard aggressively marketed her "Perspective Sketch" to American educators, believing it to be a crucial break with other materials on the market. As she confidently expressed to a friend in 1844, "In history I have *quote* invented the map". She also advocated for her "map of time" as a teaching device because she strongly believed the visual preceded the verbal, that information presented to students in graphic terms would facilitate memorization, attaching images to the mind through the eyes.

.......................................................................................

Now, onto the questions! A good understanding of a passage does not guarantee a strong performance on the questions. You will need to be detail-oriented, manage your time well, and prioritize the questions wisely no matter how well you understood the text. Again, even if you don't fully understand the passage, you can still do well with the questions if you stay calm and approach the questions strategically.

**Firstly, you don't necessarily want to complete the questions in order.** If your understanding of a passage is a little weak, you shouldn't answer a main purpose question right away (which is usually one of the earlier questions). You'll want to avoid the larger, big-picture questions that require a deeper understanding of the overall passage. Look for vocab.-in-context questions, line reference questions, and specific detail questions that you can easily locate. Every time you revisit the passage to answer these questions, your overall understanding of the passage will grow and then you'll be better prepared to answer those overarching questions.

If a question asks you to recall a detail that you can't immediately locate, don't skim the passage for it right away. Keep it on the back-burner. It's likely you'll come across it when you're looking for the answer to a separate question. After you have answered the questions you feel confident answering, you may be left with one or two of those detail questions. This is a good time to check the clock. If you've already spent your allotted time on the passage, you will want to move on.

If you have some time remaining to search for those details, **skim effectively by reading the first and last sentences of each paragraph**. *Many* of the answers to detail questions can be found in those lines (or the lines close by). By skimming this way, your eye is very likely to catch a word or phrase that will help you locate the answer. Those opening/closing lines will also give you a sense of what that particular paragraph is about and whether or not you can expect to find your answer there. If a question asks you about the *benefits* of a particular drug and the first sentence of a paragraph focuses on the *negative* side effects, the answer to the question probably won't be located in that paragraph and you can move along.

**Skip around.** There's no time to re-skim the passage for every question, so you'll have to figure out which ones to table and come back to. This is especially important if you are running low on time. We will talk about time management a bit more later.

**Pay close attention to what the question is asking!** This can't be emphasized enough. Circle key words in the question that will help you pinpoint exactly what it's asking for. Make sure that whatever answer you select isn't just a true statement, but a true statement that's relevant to the question.

**Rely on the process of elimination**. You will not always get the satisfaction of reading a question and immediately locating the obviously correct answer choice. Most of the time you'll end up with your answer as a result of paring your options down. Cross out the answer choices that are:

- True statements that do not answer the question
- Too harshly, boldly, or definitively worded (more on that later) -Partly or wholly incorrect (not supported by the passage)

**Knowing what's wrong about an answer choice is just as important as identifying what's right!** Do not focus solely on what makes an answer choice good. The test will purposely bait you with answer choices that are *mostly* good in hopes that you will ignore a problem. Don't fall into that trap! You should always be looking to <u>sniff out what those problems are and use that as a means of eliminating the answer choice right away.</u>

Sometimes the meaning behind the answer choice is correct, but the way it's worded is problematic. **Don't ignore those issues. Very harshly worded answer choices are typically not correct** . This is especially true for characterization questions. If you are asked to characterize a person in a story, you may be able to determine whether the answer should have a positive or negative connotation. But to what extreme? If a character is said to be standoffish and cold, we wouldn't want to select an answer choice that contains a word like "cruel." That language is far too bold for this scenario.

**Definitively worded answer choices – ones that contain words like "never" or "always" – should typically be avoided**. This is especially true for any science-based discussions. Scientists will very rarely speak in definitive terms.

...........................................................................................................................................

**Avoid drawing your own conclusions**. It's important that you base your decisions off of **evidence from the text** and the *reasonable* inferences that can be made. Many questions may even begin with the phrase "what can reasonably be inferred." That may mean that the answer is not *directly* stated in the text, but that there is still **sufficient evidence** to back your answer. You should **not have to connect too many dots or make conclusions entirely on your own.**

For example, if the text claims that infants typically learn to walk when they are between 11 and 15 months old, we can infer that infants usually cannot walk before they are 11 months old. Even though that wasn't stated for us directly, we can logically conclude that based on the evidence provided. What we don't want to do is start a string of thoughts that are not rooted in the facts present. Avoid the "wellll, this *probably* leads to this….and then that *could* mean this…which could *also* mean…" train of thought.

Lastly, fall **back on your general dos and don'ts for the different question types.** We will discuss these in greater detail momentarily. Having these strategic, almost rule-based approaches to the questions will make them feel less subjective. These questions are not meant to be subjective: the information in the passage combined with the overall rules for the exam is all you need to confidently arrive at the correct answer.

## MAIN PURPOSE/CENTRAL IDEA QUESTIONS

You will see a handful of these on every exam. They tend to cause students a great deal of stress, but they shouldn't! You don't have to understand a passage in order to answer these questions correctly. Your job is not to interpret the text; your job is simply to identify what the passage is about and how the information was relayed.

If you have marked up the passage, look at the circled or underlined information and read any notes that you've written down. Think about what the major talking points were. You may remember from our discussion of question prioritization that main purpose questions may not be the best ones to answer right away. In answering the other questions, you will get a real sense for what the main idea of the passage was.

Sometimes you will be asked about the main purpose of the entire passage, and sometimes you will asked about the main purpose of a single paragraph. The strategy is the same for either type of question: identify the **overall** idea. That means **avoiding specifics**. An extremely detailed answer is not going to touch on the main idea; even if the answer choice is true, it <u>doesn't answer the question</u> of what the MAIN idea is, so it must be eliminated. This circles back to the idea of eliminating true statements that do not answer the question.

If an answer choice focuses on information that was only presented halfway through or towards the end of a passage, that is also pretty safe grounds for elimination. Something that was only discussed for a small portion of a passage is not going to touch on the overall idea.

It's not enough to identify the topic of the passage. You must think about <u>how</u> the information is presented to you. **Pay close attention to words like "summary," "analysis," "critique," and "description" in the answer choices.** These words tend to get glossed over, but they are important! There is a big difference between a summary and analysis.  A summary restates information in a concise manner, while an analysis breaks a topic down on a deeper level.

### Do's

- Save this question for last if your understanding of the passage is weak
- Use your annotations to identify the overall talking points
- Pay close attention to the wording of the answer choices

### Don'ts

- Pick specific, detail-oriented answers
- Select answers that reference information introduced towards the middle/end of the passage

## VOCAB-IN-CONTEXT QUESTIONS

These questions will refer you back to a particular line in the passage and ask you how a word or phrase is being used.

These are called vocab-**in-context** for a reason! These questions are <u>not designed to test your pre-existing knowledge of the word.</u>  In fact, basing these questions off your knowledge of the word will usually get you into trouble. You must **base your decision solely on how the word or phrase is being used in this <u>unique</u> situation.** The word might be used in a way that you wouldn't typically think of, and that's okay! Let the situation guide your decision, even if it means using the original word in an unfamiliar way.

The most obvious synonym is usually not correct. Sometimes an obvious synonym may work; if the situation calls for it, don't be afraid to select it. As long as it was the <u>situation</u> that led you to that synonym and not your knowledge of the original word's definition.

**Read the sentences before and after** the line reference to give yourself those important contextual clues. The sentence containing the word alone won't always give you a strong sense for what point is being made. Reading <u>around</u> the site of the word will help build a stronger understanding of the underlying argument. Once you have that understanding, **pick your own synonym** before looking at the answer choices. The word or phrase you pick doesn't have to be formal language or grammatically correct for the sentence; just find a way to illustrate the idea in your own words. *Then* look at the provided synonyms and pick the one that most closely lines up with your own phrasing.

Be picky with the slight differences in answer choices: those minor differences can have <u>major</u> implications. Words can have very similar meanings but be used in very different ways. Synonyms can be interchangeable in some circumstances, but not in others. For example, you can call a Ferrari valuable or expensive: "valuable" and "expensive" both indicate monetary worth in this scenario. You can also refer to time spent with family as "valuable." You can't, however, refer to time spent with family as "expensive." "Valuable" can be applied to a variety of situations, but "expensive" is used exclusively in relation to cost.

**Do not default to selecting a synonym just because you're familiar with it.** If you know it doesn't really work for this situation, you should use that as a reason to <u>eliminate it.</u>  Remember how important the process of elimination is on this exam; these questions are no exception. You're safer choosing a word you're unfamiliar with than one you are familiar with that simply doesn't work for the given line reference.

If you're really stuck, try **substituting in the answer choices**. One of them should maintain the original meaning of the sentence better than the others.

Word choice will always come down to the specific situation at hand. That is ultimately what should direct your decision-making.

**Do's**

- Read before and after the specific line reference
- Pick your own synonym based on the specific situation
- Pay close attention to the minor differences in the answer choices
- Substitute in the answer choices

**Don'ts**

- Base your decision solely off the word's common definition
- Select a synonym just because it's familiar to you
- Be afraid of synonyms that use the original word in an "unusual" or unfamiliar way

........................................................................................................................................................

## DETAIL EXTRACTION QUESTIONS

A large handful of questions will simply ask you to extract or paraphrase information from the text. If you have actively marked up your document, locating the answer to these questions shouldn't be too difficult. If you have not marked up the text or your markings are not helping you to locate where this information is, remember that you don't have to answer this question right away; you can keep it on the backburner.

By nature, some of these questions are easier to find than others: the topic of the question may send you back to a very *particular* place in the passage. Others may seem like they could have been introduced at *any* point in the passage and will be harder to locate as a result. No matter what, you should be revisiting the passage to answer these questions. **Do not rely on your memory**.

**Be very detail-oriented when revisiting the passage.** Now is not the time to skim! You want to read the passage and answer choices very precisely to make sure they are lining up. You cannot simply match words in the passage to words in the answer choices and assume that they are saying the same thing. You may miss crucial language and contextual clues if you work through these questions too quickly.

Do not default to selecting an answer choice because it contains language that was found close to the site of the question. Information that's nearby might have nothing to do with the actual question! The exam will try to use "bait language" in hopes that you will select an answer choice without actually reading how that language is being used. Avoid these traps by reading carefully.

**Do's**

- Answer right away if you feel you can easily locate your proof
- Find evidence from the passage

- Reread the passage and the answer choices carefully

## Don'ts

- Answer right away if you have no idea where to look for your proof
- Rely solely on your memory of the passage
- Select answers solely because they contain language similar (or identical) to the passage without considering context

# MANAGE YOUR TIME

With 35 minutes to complete four passages, you'll have about 8.5 minutes per passage. Take that statement with a grain of salt. Some passages may take a little more time, and others a little less.

**About 3–4 minutes of that time should be spent reading through the actual text**, with the remaining time spent on the questions. As we mentioned earlier, there is no one-size-fits all reading strategy. You may find reading quickly so that you can devote more time to the questions is beneficial for you. Or you may find that a slightly slower read will help you grasp a bit more information and help you work through the questions more confidently. Figure out what works best for you.

Here is a general time management tactic:

Minutes 0–3/4: read and mark up the text

Minutes 3/4–6/7: work through the questions whose answers are easy to locate (vocab-in-context, line reference questions, certain detail-extraction questions)

Minutes 6/7–7/8: circle back to bigger-picture questions like main purpose questions

Minutes 7/8–8.5: skim the first and last lines of each paragraph in search of any remaining detail-extraction questions

...........................................................................................

**The one exception to this format is the paired passage**, in which you are presented two smaller excerpts. For this passage, you should read the first excerpt and then immediately go to the questions that deal exclusively with that excerpt (the ACT is kind enough to separate the questions for you). Once you have completed those questions, read the second excerpt and answer the remaining questions; some will be exclusively about the second excerpt and some will require you to compare and contrast the two texts. Even if you do not feel super confident in your ability to compare/contrast, there are plenty of excerpt-specific questions that you can tackle on these passage types!

...........................................................................................

You may find that you're more comfortable spending 9-10 minutes on the first 3 passages so that you can answer the questions more effectively. That would leave you with only 5-6 minutes for the last passage. If that's the case, be sure to skim the passage even quicker than normal – you don't want to spend half of your remaining time reading! Utilize the I.F.L.C strategy: read the intro, first and last sentence of each paragraph, conclusion.  Find short questions that you think you can answer quickly: line reference, vocab questions, really anything that you can do without having much knowledge of the passage.

Ideally, you'll be able to give yourself enough time to work through all 4, but realistically that won't always be the case. You will need to practice a lot and maybe build up to a point where you can do all 4, **but no matter what, you should be keeping an eye on the clock**. You will need to determine what point to cut off a passage and move onto the next. **Don't make the mistake of waiting too long before you check the time**.  It can be really easy to accidentally spend 12 minutes on a passage. That mistake can be really costly, not just shortening your time on the last passage, but the last 2, which is a hard hole to dig yourself out of.

Reading is an essential skill not only for life but for the ACT. That said, the reading on the ACT is very different from casual reading. This kind of active and attentive reading you need for the ACT differs greatly from the laid back style you would normally use when reading for leisure. Overall, you want to make sure to focus on looking for the information that you will likely be tested on. This typically centers around the **topic** of the passage, the **main point** of the passage, and the **tone** of the passage. That said, there are nuances to different passage types that necessitates a different style. Let's go through some different passage types and how to read them.

........................................................................................................................................................

## PROSE FICTION/LITERARY NARRATIVE

For these passages, you will need a slightly different approach. A prose passage is an excerpt pulled from a novel or short story. As mentioned earlier, you will likely be asked questions pertaining to the plot of the passage, so be sure to pay close attention to the plot-driven elements. Who are the characters? What are they doing? Why are they doing it? Since these passages are fiction, they will not possess the kinds of factual information and questions you would find in a passage about whales, economics, or psychology.

Besides the basic plot, you should make sure to look out for the **feelings, emotion**, and **personality traits** present in the passage. Is one character mad at another? Does someone have a peculiar trait or way of doing things? Is someone hopeful that something might happen? Scared of a certain outcome? Excited about a new adventure or change? These are the kinds of questions you want to be able to answer after reading a prose passage.

Here is an example of a prose passage you might find on the ACT. Read this passage actively as if you were taking the real test. Give yourself a few minutes to read the passage and try to pull out the feelings/emotions involved. In the space provided jot down some notes as an exercise.

## EXERCISE: PASSAGE UNDERSTANDING- PROSE FICTION

Amory Blaine inherited from his mother every trait, except one or two few, that made him worthwhile. His father, Stephen, was a useless, inarticulate man with an odd taste for the poetry of Lord Byron and a habit of drowsing over the Encyclopedia Britannica. Stephen became wealthy at thirty, when his two elder brothers, successful Chicago brokers, died. In the first flush of feeling that the world was his, Amory's father went to

Bar Harbor and met Beatrice O'Hara, and they later wed. Stephen Blaine handed down to posterity his height of just under six feet and his tendency to hesitate at crucial life moments; both of these two traits appeared in Amory. For many years, Stephen hovered in the background of his family's life, an unassertive figure with a face half-obscured by lifeless, silky hair, continually occupied in "taking care" of his wife, and continually harassed by the idea that he didn't, and couldn't, understand her.

But Beatrice Blaine! There was a woman! Early pictures taken on her father's estate at Lake Geneva, Wisconsin, or in Rome a t the Sacred Heart Convent--an educational extravagance that in her youth was only for the daughters of the exceptionally wealthy--showed the exquisite delicacy of her features, the classic artfulness and simplicity of her clothes. A brilliant education she had: her youth passed in renaissance glory, she was versed in the latest gossip of the old families of Rome; and known by name as a fabulously wealthy American girl to Cardinal Vitori and Queen Margherita and other more subtle celebrities. She learned in England to prefer whiskey and soda over w ine, and her small talk was broadened during a winter in Vienna. All in all, Beatrice O'Hara absorbed the sort of education that will be quite impossible to attain ever again: a tutelage measured by the number of things and people one could simultaneously look down on and be charming about; a culture rich in all arts and traditions, but barren of all ideas.

In her more down to earth moments, Beatrice returned to America, met Stephen Blaine and married him--this almost entirely because she was a little bit weary, a little bit sad. Her only child was carried through a tiresome season and brought into the world on a  spring day in 1896.

When Amory was five he was already a delightful companion for her. He was an auburn-haired boy, with great, handsome eyes which he would grow into eventually, an easy, imaginative mind and a taste for costumes. From his fourth to his tenth years, he saw the country with his mother in her father's private car; they went from Coronado, where his mother became so bored that she had a nervous breakdown in a fashionable hotel, down to Mexico City, where she developed an almost epidemic case of tuberculosis.

So, while more or less fortunate little rich boys were defying governesses on the beach at Newport, or being spanked or tutored or read to from young boys' classic story books, Amory was biting obliging bell-boys in the Waldorf-Astoria Hotel, outgrowing a natural disgust of chamber music and symphonies, and acquiring a highly specialized education from his mother.

"Amory."

"Yes, Beatrice." (Such a quaint name for his mother; she encouraged it.)

"Dear, *don't think* of getting out of bed yet. I've always suspected that early rising in early life makes one nervous. Clothilde is having your breakfast brought up."

"All right."

"I am feeling very old to-day, Amory," she would say, sighing, her face a rare portrait of emotion, her voice carefully controlled, her hands as poised as Sarah Bernhardt's 1 . "My nerves are on edge-- on edge. We must leave this terrifying place to-morrow and go searching for sunshine."

Amory's penetrating green eyes would look out     through his tangled hair at his mother. Even at this age he wasn't fooled by her.

"Amory."

"Oh, yes..."

"I want you to take a red-hot bath, as hot as you can bear it, and just relax your nerves. You can read in the tub if you wish."

She fed him the works of the Romantic Symbolists before he was ten; at eleven he could talk casually, if rather sentimentally, of Brahms and Mozart and Beethoven. One afternoon, when left alone in the hotel at Hot Springs, Amory sampled his mother's apricot cordial, and as the taste pleased him, he became quite tipsy. This was fun for a while, but then he spied a cigarette in his intoxication, and experienced a vulgar, common physical reaction to the drink and smoke. Though this incident horrified Beatrice, it also secretly amused her, and the story become part of her regular repertoire.

"This son of mine," he heard her tell a room full of awestruck, admiring women one day, "is entirely sophisticated and quite c harming--but delicate--we're all delicate; *here* , you know." Her hand was radiantly outlined against her beautiful bosom; then sinking her voice to a whisper, she told them of the apricot cordial. They were highly amused, for she was a brave raconteuse 2 , but many keys were turned in sideboard locks that night against the possible sneakiness of the ladies' own devils.

[1] *Sarah Bernhardt was a famous French actress of this time.*

[2] *a female storyteller*

**Describe the plot of this passage:**

_____

_____

_____


**What are the emotions, feelings, or personality involved in the passage?**

_____

_____

_____


This passage is nothing more than an introspective into the upbringing of both a mother and a child. The passage centers around a mother, Beatrice, who is well educated and affluent. She has a child, Amory, who is also well educated and peculiar. The passage delves into their interactions and personality. They find great companionship in each other as Beatrice does not find that companionship with her husband and the father of Amory, Stephen.


What you would want to understand from this passage is that Beatrice is extremely affluent and well-traveled. She was educated across the globe. She is passing that lifestyle down to her child, Amory, and their interactions are depicted as amusing and relaxed. He refers to his mother by her first name - Beatrice - rather than "mom." At one point, the young Amory takes a sip of alcohol and his mother uses it as an amusing story with her friends, where most parents might be livid at the idea of a 10 year old taking a drink. This casual and peculiar relationship between the two characters would undoubtedly be the center of most of the questions. You could expect to see several questions about the characters' interactions, the nature of the relationships, and the personalities involved.

## NONFICTION PASSAGES

As discussed earlier, there will be three nonfiction passages on the ACT. When reading these types of passages, you want to make sure to identify the **topic** in the first few paragraphs. Once you determine the topic of the work, you then want to make sure to figure out what the **main point** is. Besides those two basic things to look for, you want to try to analyze the **author's tone and perspective**. This is important because it will frame many of the answers to the questions. Some popular tones on the ACT are critical, supportive, informative (neutral), excited, questioning, and nostalgic. The author's perspective is sometimes related to the tone. This is the author's **point of view** – what the situation looks like from where the author is standing. This can be important to understand the author's **motivation** and **position** in the grand scheme of the passage. When there are multiple names mentioned in a passage, it is important to **keep track of who plays what role**.

For these next few passages, try to pull out the **topic, main point, tone,** and **perspective.**

# EXERCISE: PASSAGE UNDERSTANDING (NON- FICTION)

## Early Travel in the US

Prior to the advent of railroad transportation, people and goods traveled by animal-drawn wagons on turnpike roads. Beginning in the early 1800s, passenger travel to and from the ports and cities on both sides of the United States was accomplished by way of the National Road, a series of interconnected roadways linking major hubs. Later that same century, the Transcontinental Railway was constructed, which saved time and provided greater comfort during one's journey. Even so, travel was still a long way from being anything but a trying, exhausting experience.

The National Road's turnpikes were the 19th century equivalent of today's highways and stagecoaches were the equivalent of modern taxi cabs and buses. Together, they carried Americans across the country in the pre-railroad era. Stagecoach travel along bumpy, unpaved roads led some travelers to compare it to being "tossed in a blanket," with travelers often suffering head injuries from being thrown against the roof of the coach. Even short journeys over these roads left travelers physically exhausted and sometimes injured.

One traveler described his journey while crossing the Allegheny Mountains in 1847: "Our extensive vehicle had a significant inconvenience: it was impossible to lose sight of the absolute necessity for holding on. The great object was to prevent our heads coming in contact with the roof of the carriage, when any particularly violent jolt threw us with merciless force into the air...to be obliged to hold on with all our force to the seat, throughout the entire day, for fear of having our heads knocked in, was rather too much of a traveling inconvenience. We suffered nothing but great fatigue...I truly believe all the stories ofconcussion of the brain and other frightful misadventures connected with traveling across the mountains."

The kind of harrowing experience quoted here made the development of a quicker, more efficient, and less exhausting method of travel urgently necessary. Beginning in the 1860s, the US government funded the private construction of the Transcontinental Railroad, which would link smaller railroads in the east to the increasing number of towns cropping up in the central and western portions of the country. It took nearly a decade to complete. The fragmented construction saw many setbacks, including a great deal of corruption. It also saw the death of the many immigrants and freed slaves who provided the majority of the manual labor needed for such an enormous undertaking. However, the completion of the railroad was met with great excitement and enthusiasm by government officials and citizens alike.

Yet even as a considerably more efficient way to get from place to place, railroad travel still posed some discomfort and inconvenience for its passengers as well challenges for railroad managers and staff. For a journey of more than a few hours, for instance, it was necessary to develop a plan for feeding the passengers. Doing this successfully was not as simple as it may sound. Some travelers carried their food with them, but a growing number were demanding meals along the road. "Eating houses" began to appear at junction points. These were privately owned establishments adjacent to train depots. But they were often mobbed with train passengers who had a too-brief window in which to purchase and consume a meal, meaning that many simply went hungry. It was not long before the railroads understood that it was in their best interest to make major improvements in the care and feeding of passengers. They also realized that delivering better food and more civilized service could produce extra revenue.

As transcontinental railroads took shape, the railroads increased their efforts to provide better meals, especially for those on extended journeys. By the late 1850s, travelers could book a trip from New Orleans to

New York on a combined river steamer and railroad route. The riverboats routinely provided sleeping and dining accommodations, so the railroads felt compelled to provide comparable service to customers who were accustomed to such luxuries. As train speeds increased more and more, it became impractical to stop for meals and the dining car was born.

After its slow start, dining on a train evolved into a more elegant and, at times even romantic, experience for early cross country travelers. During the "golden age" of railroading, from the 1890s through the 1920s, it was possible to eat a meal cooked by expert chefs and served by highly skilled waiters while being whisked across picturesque landscapes by a powerful steam locomotive.

Today, however, rail travel has naturally taken a backseat to air travel. Ever in search of greater efficiency and speed, the modern traveler can't, and won't, waste days doing what can be done in hours. One can still travel from New York to San Francisco by rail, but to do it comfortably can be crippling to one's wallet, while "budget" trips can soon make one regret the cramped seating, expensive microwaved food, and the lack of bathing facilities. All of which makes flying most people's first choice when booking travel arrangements today.

**Topic** _____

**Main Point** _____
_____

**Tone** _____

**Perspective** _____

## PAIRED PASSAGES

Paired passages are reading comprehension passages where there are two separate passages (usually surrounding the same or similar issue) and then a set of 10 questions. The first few questions are about passage A, the next few about passage B, and the final few about both passages. As a reminder, the strategy here is to read passage A first, then complete the passage A questions **before** reading passage B. Then, read passage B and answer the remaining questions. In doing this, you won't accidentally muddle the two passages together before answering the questions. By reading passage A and immediately answering the questions about it, you also **solidify the topic, main point, and tone** of passage A in your mind. You can then move on to analyze passage B and treat it as a new and distinct passage from passage A.

The trick here is that the passages can have varying relationships. Sometimes they are polar opposites - one is for something, one is against it. In other instances, the passages can be in partial agreement. Even more interesting is when the passages have very little relation other than the overarching topic. It is important to go into the dual passages **considering the relationship. It is not always pure disagreement,** which is what most students expect.

It is extremely important to contemplate the relationship between the two passages. The *"dual"* passage questions at the end of the question set will surely test you on your ability to understand the difference in opinion, or lack thereof, in the two passages. You will be required to understand the interplay between the two passages and how they work together. Aside from differences in stance, you want to consider how the passages present their information: ***how* do the authors make their points?** One passage may be more personal or philosophical, and the other more factual. What types of literary devices do they use? These can be crucial similarities or differences.

Try your luck with this exercise. Read these two passages carefully and determine the topic, main point, tone, and perspective for both passages. Think about how they work together.

## Passage A

A selfie is a self-portrait taken with a smartphone. At least, that's what I assumed until two weeks ago when I stumbled on an article in *The Guardian* about the Getty Exhibition in Focus Play. "You do see self-portraits [in this photo-exhibition]," curator Arpad Kovacs said of the show, "but they are self-portraits. They are not selfies."

Instantly curious, I asked him to elaborate on the difference. He gave me a n interesting explanation. The self-portrait and selfie are two separate ways a person can create an image that defines himself. Sometimes these two ways of self-definition overlap, but not always.

Self-portraits were originally created by painters who carefully created their art. They chose the colors they used, the setting, and spent days or weeks composing the perfect portrait of who they believed themselves to be, or who they wanted to world to see them to be. A portrait is meant to be "read" as a work of art, to be studied and understood, and is intended to be a permanent record of an artist's effort.

But, to say that a portrait is permanent or "lasts" because it is better than a selfie is not necessarily correct. A portrait lasts because it was meant to. Selfies are created in a different context. Selfies are created in an instant; the actual creation happens in a push of a virtual button. A selfie is like a text; it is part of a conversation, intended to communicate an idea or a moment. As Arpad noted, "Selfies promote active discussion and responses that can be instantaneous and – more importantly – in the form of a selfie." Social media like Instagram exist so that people can converse almost entirely in images, largely selfies. These images are like text messages. Self-portraits, on the other hand, are documents. They are complex, multi-layered, and open to interpretation.

Selfies are meaningful in their social context. For example, a selfie of your best friend sitting in Starbucks is meaningful to you if you know that the cup in front of her is her favorite latte and that she's stopping there on her way to a job interview. To a stranger, she is just a woman with cup sitting in one of thousands of identical coffee shops. There is nothing to read in the image. A self-portrait, however, might be fraught with symbols and ideas embedded by the artist. A book on a shelf in the background of the portrait, for example, might tell the viewer, any viewer, that the sad smile on the subject's face comes from having just read a book of sonnets. An open window with a blowing curtain gives a hint of a spring breeze, and a tangle of flowers lying on table next to the subject suggests a rushed carelessness that begs interpretation.

To read selfies as self-portraits is to ignore their unique social purpose and in some cases to interpret them incorrectly. If, in your friend's Starbucks selfie, there happens to be a man in the background, should that person be interpreted or read as part of her image? Probably not. Selfies are not documents. Selfies may be art, but they are not necessarily self-portraits.

## Passage B

The first thing you notice when you compare a modern selfie with a historic self-portrait is what is different about them. A self-portrait painting was created following a painstaking plan. The artist likely created many preliminary sketches. He viewed himself in mirrors over and over again, experimenting with different lighting and angles. Finally, he drew and painted his image, carefully choosing the right size canvas, the perfect colors, and the right brushes to have the perfect strokes. It was an expensive process that consumed weeks and months of his time. Selfies, on the other hand, are produced within seconds with a smartphone camera, and more often than not in poor lighting, with very little planning.

So, from the outset, the two methods don't seem to have much in common. But, when we step away from *how* these images are created, and start to think more about *why* they are created, or what is the purpose of these images, it seems like they are more similar than different. The important question to ask is not, what is an individual's purpose in creating an image of herself?

Essentially, both the self-portrait and the selfie are based on the idea or wish to freeze a slice of life. So, the purpose is the same, even if how the wish is executed is vastly different. The selfie is a spontaneous or spur-of-the-moment effort to freeze that moment, while the self-portrait is planned and considered. The qualities of the two images are different, but that doesn't mean that selfies are inferior to self-portraits. That means that they have different features or can be described in different ways.

Both selfies and self-portraits reveal something about the artists who created them. Both self-portrait artists and "selfie-artists" want to capture something special. They are trying to express something they feel inside for the outside world to see. They are sharing moods, feelings, and reactions to the world around them. It is a form of intuition, or intelligence of the unconscious.

**Passage A**

| | |
|---|---|
| **Topic** | _____ |
| **Main Point** | _____ |
| | _____ |
| **Tone** | _____ |
| **Perspective** | _____ |

**Passage B**

Topic _____

Main Point _____

_____

Tone _____

Perspective _____

**How do these two passages relate?**

_____

_____

**What are the similarities and differences between the authors' opinions?**

_____

_____

································································································

## FURTHER EXERCISES

Use these remaining passages to practice your skills. Read each passage looking for the topic, main point, tone, and perspective. If it is a fiction passage, make sure to pay attention to the emotion/feeling and plot.

They had people coming to dinner: the Norman Knights (a theatre director, and she an interior decorator); a young man, Eddie Warren, who had just published a little book of poems and whom everybody was asking to dinner; and a "find" of Bertha's called Pearl Fulton. What Miss Fulton did, Bertha didn't know. They had met at the club and Bertha had felt an instant spark of sisterhood, as she always did with beautiful women who had something rare about them.

The provoking thing was that, though they met a number of times and really talked, Bertha couldn't make her out. Up to a certain point Miss Fulton was rarely, wonderfully frank, but the certain point was there, and beyond that she would not go. And this reticence intrigued Bertha all the more.

She went into the drawing room, and picking up the carefully arranged cushions one by one, she threw them back onto the chairs and the couches. The room came alive at once. As she was about to throw the last one, she surprised herself by suddenly hugging it to her, passionately. But it did not put out the warmth in her being. Oh, on the contrary!

The windows of the drawing room opened out to a balcony overlooking the garden. At the far end, there was a tall, slender pear tree in richest, fullest bloom; Bertha couldn't help feeling that it had not a single bud or a faded petal. She turned away from the window and began walking up and down. . . .

How strong the jonquils smelled in the warm room. Too strong? Oh, no. And yet, as though overcome, she flung down on a couch and pressed her hands to her eyes.

"I'm too happy—too happy!" she murmured. And she seemed to see on her eyelids the lovely pear tree with its wide open blossoms as a symbol of her own life.

Really, she had everything. She was young. Harry and she were in love and they got on together splendidly.

They didn't have to worry about money. They had this absolutely glorious house and garden. And friends: people keen on social questions, books, and music. And she had found a wonderful dressmaker, and they were going abroad in the summer, and their new cook made superb omelettes. . .

"I'm absurd. Absurd!" She sat up, but she felt quite dizzy, drunk. It must have been the spring.

She floated softly into the hall, and kissed the Norman Knights, the first to arrive. She ushered them into the drawing room. Harry came home from work, and Eddie soon joined them. And then Bertha realized that Pearl Fulton had not turned up.

"Ah! There's a taxi, now." And Bertha smiled with that little air of proprietorship that she always assumed while her women finds were still new and mysterious.

"Am I late?"

"No, not at all," said Bertha. "Come along." And she politely took her arm and they moved into the dining-room.

What was there in the touch of that cool arm that could convey the warm feeling of close friendship that Bertha sensed? Miss Fulton did not look at her. But Bertha knew, suddenly, as if the warmest look had passed between them - as if they had said to each other, "You too?" - that Pearl Fulton was feeling just what she was feeling: they were kindred spirits.

Oh, why did she feel so generous towards the whole world tonight? Everything was good - was right.

Everything seemed to fill her brimming cup of bliss.

And still, in the back of her mind, there was the pear tree. It would be silver now, silver as Miss Fulton, who sat there turning a tangerine in her slender fingers, which were so pale that a light seemed to come from them.

How she could have guessed Miss Fulton's mood so exactly, so instantly? She never doubted for a moment that she was right, and yet what had she to go on? Less than nothing.

"I believe this type of connection does happen, very rarely between women. Never between men," thought Bertha. "While I am making coffee in the drawing-room perhaps she will 'give a sign'... "

"Don't turn up the light for a moment. It is so lovely." Miss Fulton was crouched by the fire. Then in the next moment Miss Fulton "gave the sign."

"Have you a garden?" said the cool, sleepy voice. This question was so perfect on her part that all Bertha could do was to obey. She crossed the room, pulled the curtains apart, and opened the windows.

"There!" she breathed.

And the two women stood side by side looking at the slender, flowering tree. Although it was so still it seemed, like a candle flame, to stretch up, to quiver in the bright air, to grow taller as they gazed—almost to touch the round, silver moon.

How long did they stand there? Caught in that circle of unearthly light, understanding each other perfectly, kindred creatures, caught up in the moment in all this blissful treasure of friendship, kinship?

**Describe the plot of this passage**

_____

_____

_____

**What are the emotions, feelings, or personality involved in the passage?**

_____

_____

_____

## NONFICTION: CLIMATE CHANGE AND TREE SPECIES LOSS

The forests of North America have seen plenty of change in a pretty short period of time, at least geologically speaking. Up until about 18,000 years ago, the Laurentide Ice Sheet covered Canada and much of the eastern United States. When temperatures climbed and the ice sheet retreated, forests gradually reemerged. But how? Did pockets of trees find refuge in sheltered areas during the Ice Age? Or were all tree species pushed to the southern tier of the United States, only to spread north again after the ice disappeared?

Scientists still debate the topic, but one thing is clear: today's forests in the eastern United States bear little resemblance to postglacial forests. Starting with European colonial settlers and marching through four centuries of development, drought, and fire, the tree cover of North America has become fragmented. "There are hardly any forests in the eastern U.S. that have never been cleared—maybe only a small percentage," said Claire Jantz, a researcher at the Woods Hole Research Center in Falmouth, Massachusetts. But changes in temperature, precipitation, and atmospheric concentrations of carbon dioxide could eventually do as much to remake the forests as humans did with saws and fires and bulldozers.

Jantz and her colleagues have been examining the state of current forest cover in National Parks, such the Appalachian region of the United States, while also modeling what the future of these forests will look like. They have been working in the Delaware Water Gap National Recreation Area (Pennsylvania and New Jersey), Shenandoah National Park (Virginia), and Great Smoky Mountains National Park (North Carolina and Tennessee). Jantz used the output from a large number of climate models to simulate future climate conditions, which assume that carbon dioxide emissions will continue to follow the current trend—rising from 400 parts per million to 1370 parts per million by the year 2100. The climate models showed that warming would accelerate in all three parks. The average increase is about 0.7 to 0.8 °F (about 0.4 °C) per decade until 2040, after which warming will speed up to about 1.2 °F (0.7 °C) per decade.

While predictions about rising temperatures are a widespread consensus, it's harder to predict exactly what will happen in terms of precipitation. "It is entirely possible that precipitation will decrease, which would exacerbate droughts and create ideal conditions for fires," she said. "If, however, precipitation increases substantially, it could enhance growth for many trees in a warmer climate."

The parks of Appalachia, for example, should expect to see rising temperatures, along with fewer days of frost, a phenomenon which affects the length of the growing season. Precipitation is expected to increase somewhat, but also become more variable. The combination of minor precipitation increases, higher maximum temperatures in the summertime, and a lengthened growing season, mean the frequency of drought will likely increase.

By combining these climate projections with information about topography and soil moisture/composition, Jantz and her team are also exploring how suitable the future habitat may be for the growth of 40 eastern tree species. Their modeled projections are based, in part, on extensive field observations collected by the U.S. Forest Service. Jantz is combining all of this information into a comprehensive vulnerability assessment, aimed at land managers (park service staff who oversee the protection and conservation of preserved land), that is designed to facilitate planning and decision-making.

It turns out that sugar maple and eastern hemlock, which Jantz calls "iconic species of eastern U.S. forests," are expected to lose habitat. Lower elevations (those areas of land closer to sea level) and the more southerly latitudes curvebreakerstestprep.com 154 / of the east coast - which historically have provided the cool, wet habitats preferred by these species - will do so less and less as climate changes continue to take place. Other species, however, would do quite well as climate changes take place. Black-jack oak and black hickory trees are expected to gain habitat in areas that become warmer and drier. High-elevation species, like red spruce and balsam fir, may eventually be pushed off the mountains, as sea levels may rise.

The suitability of a landscape is just one factor in determining the success of a species. "If you look at the overall suitability of land, a lot of species do well," Jantz said. "But there are other reasons that trees won't set seed or reach maturity; for instance, the climate may change too quickly, or seeds won't be able to disperse and establish themselves in fragmented land. It's humbling and disconcerting to see areas where conditions for growth could improve, but the trees have little chance of getting there unless there is active management by parks and other stewards of our lands."

[1] *the arrangement of the natural and artificial physical features of an area*

**Topic** _____

**Main Point** _____

_____

**Tone** _____

**Perspective** _____

## NONFICTION: PROMISE OF AMERICAN LIFE

The average American is nothing if not patriotic. "The Americans are filled," says Mr. Emil Reich in his "Success Among the Nations," "with such an implicit and absolute confidence in their Union and in their future success that any negative remark is not acceptable. We have had many opportunities of hearing public speakers in America cast doubts upon the very existence of God, question the historic nature or truth of the whole fabric of Christianity. But never have we caught the slightest whisper of doubt, the slightest want of faith, in America—unlimited belief in the future of America."

The faith of Americans in our own country, which is practically religious, pervades the air we breathe. As children we hear it asserted or implied in the conversation of our elders. Every new stage of our educational training provides some additional testimony on its behalf. Newspapers and novelists, orators and playwrights, even if they are little else, are at least loyal preachers of the Truth. We may distrust and dislike much that is done in the name of our country by our fellow-countrymen; but our country itself, its democratic system, and its prosperous future are above suspicion.

When Americans talk of their country as the Land of Promise, a question is raised as to precisely what they mean. They mean, in general, that the future will have something better in store for them individually and collectively than has the past or the present. What are the benefits which this better future will give to Americans either individually or as a nation? And how is this Promise to be fulfilled? Will it fulfill itself, or does it imply certain responsibilities? If so, what responsibilities? When we speak of a young man's career as promising, we mean that he has the ability and opportunity to become rich or famous or powerful. This judgment does not imply any responsibility. It is merely a prophecy based upon the young man's past performances and qualities. But the career becomes for the young man himself a serious task.

For him, the better future will not merely happen. He will have to do something to deserve it. It may be wrecked by unforeseen obstacles, by unsuspected sicknesses, or by some critical error of judgment.

So it is with the Promise of American life. From the point of view of an immigrant, this Promise may consist of the anticipation of a better future, which he can share merely by taking up his residence on American soil. But once he has become an American, the Promise can no longer be an anticipation, or a hope. It becomes a responsibility, which requires a certain kind of behavior on the part of himself and his fellow-Americans. And when we attempt to define the Promise of American life, we must also describe the kind of behavior which the fulfillment of the Promise demands.

This vision of a better future is not as clear for the present generation of Americans as it was for former generations. But, our country still figures in the imagination of its citizens as the Land of Promise. They still believe that somehow, sometime, something better will happen to good Americans than has happened to men in any other country. This belief is an essential part of our national ideal. From the beginning, Americans have been anticipating and imagining a better future. From the beginning, the Land of Democracy has been a Land of Promise. In cherishing the Promise of a better national future, Americans are fulfilling the national tradition.

The only fruitful promise that an individual or any nation can have is a promise determined by an ideal. Several European nations have a specific purpose determined for the most part by the pressure of historical circumstances. However, the American nation is committed to a purpose that is not just related to history. It is committed to the realization of the democratic ideal; and if its Promise is to be fulfilled, it must be prepared to follow wherever that ideal may lead.

As much as we may dislike the American personality that takes the fulfillment of our national Promise for granted, the American belief in the ideal Promise demands respectful consideration. It has its roots in the conditions of American life, and in the actual experience of the American people.

**Topic** _____

**Main Point** _____

**Tone** _____

**Perspective** _____

# SUMMARY

- Spend the time on the questions that are most likely to award you points.

- Understand the passage types and how they differ.

- Understand the time structure of the exam and how many minutes you have per question and per passage.

- Understand common question types (main purpose, vocab.-in-context, detail extraction, etc.)

- Prioritize the passages – do the "easiest" passage first.

- Make sure to read the introductory blurb at the top of the passage.

- Read the passage next, annotating wisely.

- Make sure to focus intensely on the intro, conclusion, and first and last sentence of each paragraph.

- Make a roadmap of the passage while you read it.

- For Fiction passages, look for plot, character traits, and feelings/emotions.

- For nonfiction passages, look for topic, main point, tone, structure, and perspective.

- Take a moment after reading to digest the overall idea of the passage.

- Consider completing line reference questions first to build understanding.

- Consider completing "global" questions, like main idea questions, last.

- Pay close attention to the question stem and what the question is asking.

- Rely on the process of elimination.

- Nitpick words in the choices to eliminate statements that don't match the tone or style of the passage.

- For vocab-in-context questions, base your decision solely on how the word is being used in the situation (and not on its typical definition).

- Replace the vocab-in-context word with a synonym of your own choosing, then try to match it with a choice. As a last resort try substituting in answer choices.

- For main purpose questions, avoid specifics and pay close attention to words like "summary," "critique," and "analysis"

- Consider reading sentences before and after any line reference or vocab -in-context

- Be detail-oriented when revisiting the passage for detail-extraction questions. Don't get fooled by bait language.

- For paired passages, reading Passage A and then immediately answer the Passage A questions. Then move on to Passage B and the remaining questions.

- Do not draw your own conclusions. Find some level of evidence (even if it's not direct) to support your answers. Reasonable inferences should not require connecting too many dots.

- Make sure you keep an eye on the clock throughout the section. Do not wait until you are on the last passage to check your time.

# ACT SCIENCE

·······································································································································

## WHAT'S THE GIST?

The science section is the final portion of the exam. You will have **35 minutes** to complete **40 questions**. You will have either six or seven passages to work through (each consisting of anywhere between five and seven questions).

Each question is a multiple choice question with four possible answer choices. You are **not allowed to use your calculator for this section**, so you may need to do some simple arithmetic by hand.

## WHAT CAN YOU EXPECT TO SEE?

The type of passages you will see will differ from one exam to another. Unlike the reading section, there is not a set order to the passages, but you can expect to see the following:

- **2-3 Data Representation Passages** (about 12–15 questions): Understand, evaluate, and interpret information presented in graphs, tables, and charts

    - Common questions include tracing/locating values directly from a graph or chart, reading "between" measurements to predict a value, reading "beyond" a graph/ table to predict a value, and using multiple graphs/charts/tables to draw a conclusion

- **2-3 Research Summaries Passages** (about 18–22 questions): Interpret and analyze the design or results of one or several studies

    - Common questions include determining the dependent (observed) and independent (controlled) variables in an experiment, establishing a relationship between variables (direct vs. indirect, linear vs. nonlinear), determining why certain steps in a procedure were carried out, understanding how changes to the design of the experiment will affect its outcome, and drawing conclusions from the information/ data represented

- **1 Conflicting Viewpoints Passage** (about 6–8 questions): Compare, contrast, and analyze opposing theories or hypotheses

- Common questions include determining if a statement will weaken/strengthen one or more of the arguments, determining whether one or more scientists would agree/disagree with a statement based on their stances, and analyzing the fundamental differences between multiple theories

# STRATEGIES

The science section isn't really about the science! Don't panic if you don't remember every little detail; you don't need to. **The science section can be thought of as reading comprehension with the addition of graphs and figures.** The difficulty with this section usually comes down to not being familiar with how to actually work through the passages. You've had a lot of practice over the years with regular reading comprehension, but this style of data-driven reading comprehension is a little new.

We will discuss some general strategies for how to quickly read through the passages and identify the important pieces of information. There simply isn't enough time to read each word carefully, **so being able to zero in on what's important is key**. That's really what this section is all about: determining what's important, making connections, drawing some reasonable conclusions, and being detail-oriented. It's not about the actual science, so **don't get lost in the science part of the "science" section.**

That being said, although this section does not *rely* on your science knowledge, **there are some questions that will require you to know some basic scientific principles** (and even some mathematical ones – you may be required to balance an equation using proportions, calculate percentages, or convert units). Be sure to brush up on those mathematical techniques in addition to solidifying those core scientific principles. We'll discuss those basics later on.

As we mentioned before, there are three general passage types: **1)** data representation passages, **2)** research-based passages, **3)** and conflicting viewpoints passages.

The **data representation passages** are usually the briefest and contain information about something that scientists or students observed. There are recorded values associated with these observations, from which we can maybe draw some conclusions about the topic at hand.

The **research-based passages** contain actual physical experiments that were performed. Usually there are several different studies within one passage that all deal in one way or another with the topic the scientists or students were studying.

The **conflicting viewpoints passage** presents two or more hypotheses on a topic. These are usually the most time consuming and the most challenging of the passages. For that reason, you may want to leave this passage to last, which brings us to our first general strategy.

**You don't have to read the passages in order. Prioritize the passages you think are easier.** With extensive practice, you'll become skilled at identifying if a passage is going to be straightforward or not. If the passage doesn't contain a lot of text, it's probably a more straightforward passage. If the questions are short and the answer choices are mostly numerical, it's likely that the passage contains several direct, graph-reading questions. **The passages do not increase in difficulty toward the end,** and as we noted earlier, there is no set order to the type of passages like there is in the reading section. So you may want to hop around a bit.

The questions *within* **a passage DO tend to get more challenging closer to the end**, though. There are usually about five to six questions per passage and the first 2–3 are typically the most straightforward. Don't overthink these. The final one or two questions in each passage usually require a deeper understanding of the passage. You may have to relate multiple experiments with one another to draw a conclusion, relate the textual information with the graphical information, and you're not always told where to look for the answers. **Do not get stuck on these questions!** You need to manage your time very wisely on the science section. For every minute you spend on a super challenging question that you may never fully understand, you're robbing yourself of time you can spend on some of the simpler questions. **Prioritize the "easier" questions, especially if you're short on time**.

So now let's discuss how to actually read through the passages. **In general, you do not want to completely skip over the passage**. Some students will go straight to the questions, but that's not useful, especially for the trickier passages. You want to **quickly skim through the passages** to get an idea of:

- What is being studied/observed?
- For what purpose is the experiment being done?
- What do the variables represent? You should circle the variables and what they stand for.
- A loose idea of how the experiment is performed (emphasis on loose, you do not want to get caught up reading the specifics here. Just know where the description of the experiment's setup is so that you can refer back to it as needed).
- What is represented on the graphs? Reading the titles and axes can give you an idea of what that experiment entailed and how it differs from the other experiments within the passage.
- Make note of any formulas or italicized language.

The **visuals are arguably the most important part of a passage,** so be sure to pay close attention to the graphs, tables, figures, and diagrams. We will discuss general graph reading skills, how graphs help us differentiate studies, and how the relationship between variables is determined through graphs/tables later on.

Let's go over some general strategies to help you tackle the questions. The questions tend not to be overly-complicated; they just *seem* that way. When you're presented with a lot of information at once, it can be overwhelming. That, paired with the scientific language, can make even the simplest of questions appear intimidating. As a result, it's useful to **simplify the question by rephrasing it in your own words and breaking the ideas apart.**

**You can deal with the question in pieces**. You can even start looking for values before you finish reading the question! Before you can draw a conclusion, you have to do your research first. **Go *find* your important values** before you worry about how you're meant to *use* those values.

**Mark up the important elements in the question**. Numbers, variables, materials, dates –anything that helps to identify important information should be circled. You'll want to start looking at the graphs once you find these important terms and **mark those graphs up** *while* **you're reading the question.**

**Annotating the questions and annotating the figures at the same time** can also really limit careless mistakes, like reading the wrong curve, axis, or even the wrong graph. Simple questions can still be a challenge because they're prone to careless mistakes, **so use your pencil actively to avoid these mishaps.** Start by making sure you **refer to the correct figure** when it's specified which one to use.

When a question does not direct you to a specific table/chart, it might seem difficult to figure out where to locate the necessary information. Luckily **there are clues built into the question** (and answer choices) that can help.

- When you spot the phrase **"according to the passage"** or **"based on the description of the experiment,"** you will likely need to refer back to the introductory text or the steps describing the physical design of an experiment

- If it's a question pertaining to how the experiment was carried out or asks why the students/scientists performed a certain step, **refer to the description of the experiment**

    - **Note:** when you are asked why an action is carried out, think back to the important factors of the experiment. If heat, for example, is a large component of an experiment and you are asked why the scientists performed a certain task, it's likely that the answer choice has something to do with heat. Even if you don't understand the mechanics behind the answer, you can still **arrive at the correct answer by picking the one that pairs with an important element of the experiment.**

- When a question prompts you to consider the **"outcome of the experiments"** or refers you to "studies 1-3," you will need to connect some dots. The answer will not be found in a single place. You will likely need to **find some underlying pattern** or use the findings in one study in connection with the findings in another study to **draw a conclusion.**

- When you think the necessary information can be found in the figures, but are not sure which graph/table to look at, focus on the specifics of the question. If you've actively marked it up, you'll have circled some **key terms that will help you pair it with a figure**. Pay close attention to units! If you're unsure which axes represent which variables, the **units will help you properly pair the answers** (or question prompts) with the correct graph and axis.

- If you read a question and cannot piece together what information will help you make a conclusion, take a look at the answer choices. They will often refer to specific features (graphs, groups, names, etc.) that can help you figure out where to look. This is especially important for questions containing two-sided answers with justifications.

Let's discuss those two-sided questions in greater detail. These are questions where you are provided **two opposite answers to select from** (Yes/No, More/Less, Higher/Lower) and **different justifications** to prove the answer. Those justifications are tools that will help you better understand the question and determine where the important information can be found in the passage. They can also help you narrow down the answers to two choices. Even with no understanding of the question itself, you can typically give yourself 50/50 chances of answering these questions correctly by **eliminating the two answers that are not supported by the graphs/data.** The justifications provided will simply not line up with the information in the passage.

Let's say one of the answer choices is "Yes. The highest survival rate occurred when the pH value was at its lowest." If you look at the relevant graph, and you see that the highest survival rate does **not** occur when the pH value was lowest, you can eliminate that answer. It is very likely that there will be another answer choice like this one that provides a false justification.

Justifications may also be eliminated if they go against a core scientific principle. If the justification includes something that is generally false (like denser items floating in a less dense liquid), you can safely eliminate those answers. **Never underestimate the power of giving yourself better odds through the process of elimination!**

Next, you must **be mindful of the set-up.** Many questions will test your understanding of the relationship between two variables by asking you to <u>complete a statement</u>. You may understand that relationship but lose points by not paying close attention to the way the statement began. Make sure that the answer you select accurately completes the statement that was begun for you.

Several questions may ask you to predict what would happen if some element of the experiment was changed. That will require you to understand how elements of the experiment affect one another. **When asked about a change to the experiment, start by determining what the result is under the CURRENT conditions.** It is extremely likely that the correct answer choice will contain that result as a reference for the new result under changed conditions. Even if you can't fully grasp the question or draw the conclusion you're intended to draw, you can pretty safely narrow it down to the answer choices that make a reference to the experiment's current results.

........................................................................................................................

Lastly, let's circle back to the **conflicting viewpoints** passage that we briefly mentioned earlier. This type of passage will require you to compare and contrast multiple viewpoints on some topic/experiment. The difficulty with these types of passages is that they will require a deeper reading of the actual text. These passages very rarely contain graph reading questions, so it will come down to your reading comprehension.

To simplify these passages, give yourself some brief notes or annotations about each student/scientist's viewpoint. Typically after you begin reading the second argument, you can start to pinpoint (and make note of) the major differences. Don't spend too much time writing; any brief notes or drawings that can help you summarize the argument will go a long way to keep you from having to reread the text several times.

**Note:** If you are short on time and you have saved this passage for last, you may not want to chew up your clock reading through all of the provided hypotheses. Take a look at the questions and see which perspectives are being referenced. If you see that several questions deal with Student 2, for example, you can simply read Student 2's stance and answer those questions before moving on to the other viewpoints.

# GRAPH READING

Graph reading is an essential skill for the science section. Several questions will simply require that you accurately pull information from the graphs and tables provided, so it's important that you feel comfortable:

- Tracing values

- Determining "in between" values (Interpolating)

- Reading "beyond" the graph (Extrapolating)

Tracing values will require you to be detail-oriented. Make sure that you **pay close attention to the axes** (use the units to help) **to ensure you are using the correct variables**. You also want to be sure that you are using the right curve when multiple curves appear on a single graph. **Be especially careful with graphs that contain multiple y-axes.** You must be sure that you are using the correct curve *and* that you trace the value back to the correct axis.

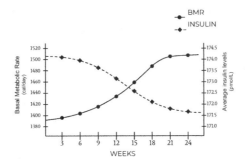

Let's say we were asked to calculate the BMR at 18 weeks. To properly identify this value, we would start by locating 18 weeks on the x-axis and tracing upward to the curve that represents BMR- in this case, the solid black line with the round markers. Carefully identifying which curve to use is only half the battle. We also have to be sure we are <u>tracing back to the correct y-axis</u> since in some cases there can be multiple.

If we are not careful, we may default to using whichever axis is the closest. In this case, that would be the y-axis on the right-hand side, which is NOT the axis representing BMR.

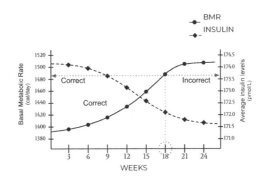

**Be mindful of your axis labels**. They are crucial to understanding the graphs. Pay special attention to words like "average" or "percent." That should change the way you think about the presented values. The number "80" on an axis that represents a percent of something does **not** mean there were 80 units of that substance.

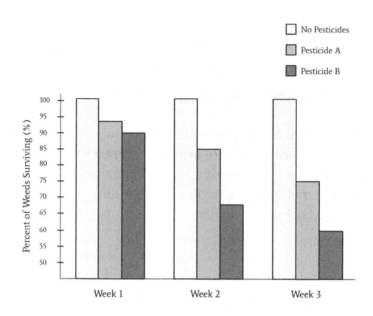

If we look closely, the y- axis represents the PERCENT of weeds that survived. The values presented do NOT represent the actual <u>number</u> of weeds surviving, but rather the <u>percent</u> of the original amount that survived. When you are presented with a graph with this type of axis, you will often be asked to evaluate an <u>amount</u> *using* the percentages and a starting value given in the question.

**Q:** Suppose a plot of land containing 300 weeds was treated with pesticide A. After 2 weeks, how many weeds would remain?

**A:** If we trace the graph, we will find that 85% of the weeds survived. This does NOT mean that the number of weeds that survived is 85. To calculate the number of surviving weeds, we need to determine 85% of our original value (300). Remember, you are not permitted a calculator, so you will need to perform this math by hand. Or you can think about it logically. 85% of 100 is 85, so 85% of 300 would be three times that amount. 3 x 85 = 255

**Note:** The graph above contained a group where no pesticide was added. **When there is a group in an experiment that remains unchanged, we often refer to it as the "control group."** It is a standard for comparison: we can determine the effects of our independent variable by comparing it to the control group, which was not affected at all by the independent variable.

........................................................................................................................

## PAIRED GRAPHS

Keep in mind that a single graph may not be enough to fully answer a question. You may need to use multiple graphs to arrive at a conclusion. You'll want to focus on what elements two graphs have in common: that provides you a link.

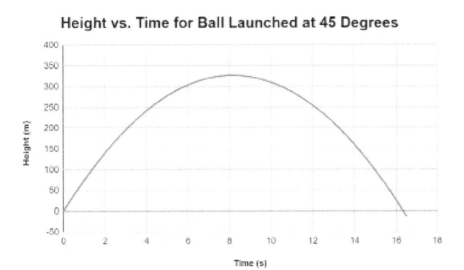

If a question asks you about the relationship between A and C, but there is no single table or graph that contains information about *both* those variables, you will need to find a bridge between separate graphs. If one graph compares A with B and a second graph compares B with C, you can use what the two graphs have in common (in this case, B) to determine the relationship you were initially asked about.

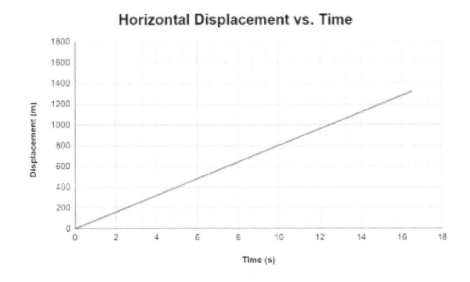

For example, the two graphs shown describe a ball in flight after being launched at a 45 degree angle from the ground. A question might ask "What is the horizontal displacement of the ball at the peak of its height?" In this case you would have to go to the first graph to determine at what time the ball

reaches that peak. Once you have this value, you can go to the second graph and match it to the horizontal displacement for that time. Your "bridge" here was time, which is the only common variable between the two graphs.

....................................................................................................................................

When a graph or table presents you with the measured values from an experiment, you can use those to estimate what would have happened if you had measured something **in between** the existing values. If you can establish the relationship between variables, you will simply need to continue the trend. Visually, this looks like drawing a line between two points whose values you know. This idea of following the trend will also help you to predict measurements **beyond** the actual measured values. Think actively about two things:

- Is the relationship direct or indirect?
- Is the relationship linear or nonlinear?

A **direct relationship** between variables indicates that when one variable increases, the other also increases (and that when one decreases, the other decreases). An **indirect relationship**, also commonly referred to as an *inverse relationship*, indicates that when one variable increases, the other decreases.

A **linear relationship** indicates that when one variable changes by a steady amount, the other variable also changes by a steady amount. The two variables don't need to be changing by the same amount as one another; it's simply important that they each grow or decline at a constant rate.

Determining whether variables have direct/indirect and linear/nonlinear relationships can also help you to:

- Turn tables into graphs

    - **Direct** relationships will have **positive** (upward facing) slopes.

    - **Inverse** relationships will have **negative** (downward facing) slopes.

    - **Linear** relationships will be represented as **lines** (hence the name).

    - **Nonlinear** relationships will be represented as **curves**.

- Answer minimization/maximization problems

    - When asked to maximize or minimize a variable, you must consider its relationship to other variables.

    - If the relationship is **direct**, you will want to **maximize one by maximizing the other**.

    - If the relationship is **indirect**, you'll want to **maximize one by *minimizing* the other**.

|          | Velocity (cm/ second) | Incline angle (degrees) | Ball diameter (mm) | Ball mass (kg) |
|----------|----------|----------|----------|----------|
| Trial 1  | 28.2 | 10 | 40 | 1.5 |
| Trial 2  | 31.5 | 15 | 40 | 1.5 |
| Trial 3  | 39.1 | 20 | 40 | 1.5 |
| Trial 4  | 48.8 | 25 | 40 | 1.5 |
| Trial 5  | 36.6 | 20 | 40 | 1.0 |
| Trial 6  | 38.1 | 20 | 40 | 1.3 |
| Trial 7  | 39.6 | 20 | 40 | 1.6 |
| Trial 8  | 41.1 | 20 | 40 | 1.9 |
| Trial 9  | 42.0 | 20 | 20 | 1.3 |
| Trial 10 | 40.2 | 20 | 30 | 1.3 |
| Trial 11 | 38.4 | 20 | 40 | 1.3 |
| Trial 12 | 36.6 | 20 | 50 | 1.3 |

**Q:** Suppose a trial was conducted with a 1.5 kg ball that had a 40-mm diameter. If the incline angle was 30 degrees, what would be the ball's velocity in cm/sec?

**A:** We currently have 4 trials that test the velocity of 1.5kg balls with 40 mm diameters: trials 1-4. The angles tested increase from 10 to 25 degrees. That means to estimate the velocity at an incline angle of 30 degrees, we'd have to read "beyond" the table. Taking a closer look, we see that velocity and incline angle have a direct relationship: when the incline angle was increased, the velocity also increased. If we follow this trend, we know that the velocity at an angle of 30 degrees would have to be greater than that at 25 degrees, so the velocity would be greater than 48.8 cm/sec.

**Q:** What would be the velocity of a 1.75 kg ball with a 40mm diameter rolled down a ramp at an angle of 20 degrees?

**A:** Trials 5-8 use mass as the independent (controlled) variable. We are given velocities for a ball weighing 1.6 kg and 1.9 kg; those velocities are 39.6 and 41.1. A ball with a mass of 1.75 kg would fall "in between" these two trials, so the velocity would be between 39.6 and 41.1.

**Q:** Graph the relationship between velocity and incline angle.

**A:** If we look at the relationship between velocity and incline angle, we see that the two variables have a direct relationship. As angle increases, velocity increases, so we know that whatever graph we choose, it must have a positive slope. The last thing we have to determine is whether or not that relationship is linear. As the incline angle increases steadily by 5 degrees, that velocity does NOT increase by a steady amount. The velocities of trials 1 and 2 differ by just over 3 cm/sec, while the velocities of trials 2 and 3 differ by more than 7. That means our relationship – and by extension, our graph –– is nonlinear. Because the differences in velocity are getting larger, the incline in our graph will get steeper.

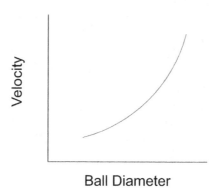

**Q:** Graph the relationship between velocity and ball diameter.

**A:** Looking at the relationship between velocity and ball diameter, we see that as the diameter increases, velocity decreases. This is an inverse (or indirect) relationship, which means our graph will have a negative slope. Our next step is to determine if the relationship is linear. As diameter increases by steady increments of 10 mm, the velocity also decreases by steady increments (of 1.8 cm/sec). That means that our relationship – and by extension, our graph – will be linear.

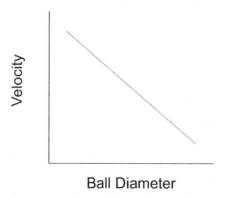

**Q:** What diameter, ball mass, and incline angle will produce the greatest velocity?

**A:** Determining what scenario will produce the greatest velocity will require us to think about velocity's relationship with each of our independent variables. Velocity had direct relationships with both incline angle and ball mass. To produce the greatest velocity, we would want to maximize both the ball mass and the incline angle. Velocity and ball diameter had an inverse relationship, so to produce the greatest velocity, we would want to minimize the diameter. The scenario with the greatest mass and incline angle, but the smallest diameter, would produce the greatest velocity.

........................................................................................................................

As we mentioned earlier, graphs are important tools in understanding which variables were at play in an experiment and in differentiating one study from another. Without needing to *read* the description of a study, you can determine which variables were controlled, which variables were measured, and how that sets it apart from another study in the experiment.

*Controlled* **variables are the** *independent* **variables in an experiment.** They are the elements that scientists/students change to monitor their effects on the dependent variables. Independent variables are found **on the x-axis** or are represented as multiple curves on a single graph.

*Dependent* **variables are the** *measured* **values that** are affected by the independent variables. Dependent variables are found on **the y-axis**.

........................................................................................................................

Keep in mind that **sometimes the graphs alone don't tell the whole story,** and they can't always distinguish one study from another. If two or more graphs look identical in terms of what information is presented – same variables on the x and y axes, same curves/keys, and no distinction in the title – you may want to **take a moment to skim through some text.** Usually the text that opens the second (and sometimes third) studies will emphasize a change in the experiment that can't be identified in the graph. Those changes (which represent another controlled parameter of the experiment) will definitely be important in understanding the overall passage.

Lastly, **graphs can very often tell us when the __actual__ measurements occurred.** Markers (usually a symbol or a shape) indicate that a measurement was recorded at that time. Curves or lines connecting those markers are __estimated__ values.

# SCIENCE BASICS

Here are some of the scientific concepts you might be required to know. Don't worry too much about memorizing everything – not many questions will require this sort of background knowledge. Of these topics, some are more commonly tested than others. The pH scale, properties of density, and prefixes are seen the most frequently.

**The pH scale:** The pH scale ranges from 1 to 14 and is used to measure the acidity/alkalinity of a solution.

- anything **under** 7 is considered **acidic**
- 7 is a **neutral** pH
- anything **over** 7 is **alkaline** (sometimes referred to as **basic**)

........................................................................................................................

**Phase change:** With an increase/decrease in temperature, matter will undergo basic phase changes (between solid, liquid, and gas).

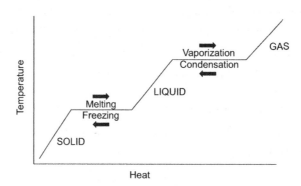

- When in doubt, think of water. When it's really cold, it turns to ice (solid). When it warms up, it melts and turns to liquid. When you boil it, it turns to steam (gas).

........................................................................................................................

**Basic unit conversions and prefixes:** The most commonly tested prefixes are kilo, centi, and milli.

| Prefix | Symbol | Meaning | Scientific Notation |
|--------|--------|---------|---------------------|
| Kilo- | k | 1,000 | $10^3$ |
| Centi- | c | .01 (one hundredth) | $10^{-2}$ |
| Milli- | m | .001 (one thousandth) | $10^{-3}$ |

Be sure you know how to convert from one unit to the other. You will need to move the decimal place to the:

- RIGHT when converting from larger unit to smaller unit
- LEFT when converting from smaller unit to larger unit

    Ex: 5L is equivalent to 5,000 mL  (moved decimal place 3 units to the right).

    30L is equivalent to .03 kL (moved decimal place 3 units to the left).

....................................................................................................

**How charges interact**: Opposite charges (positive and negative) will attract one another. Like charges (positive and positive; negative and negative) will repel one another.

....................................................................................................

**Properties and formula for density**:  Density is the ratio of an object's mass and volume.

$$D = \frac{m}{v}$$

- In a solution, objects that are **less** dense will **float**.
- Objects that are **more** dense will **sink**.

....................................................................................................

**Basic cell structure and functions**

- The cell **nucleus** acts as the brain of the cell and contains the cell's DNA (the genetic make-up from which proteins are made).
- The **mitochondria**, sometimes referred to as the powerhouse of the cell, creates energy-rich molecules (ATP) for the cell.
- The **cell membrane** holds all of the pieces of the cell together and serves as a barrier between the cell and adjacent cells.
- **Chloroplasts** only exist in plant cells and assist in the process of photosynthesis.

    ***Photosynthesis** is the process in which plants take carbon dioxide, water and sunlight and convert it into sugar (glucose) and oxygen.

### Molecular structures

- **Sugars**: $C_6H_{12}O_6$ is the basic glucose (sugar) molecule structure
- **Fats** (saturated, unsaturated and trans): are made up of C (Carbon), H (Hydrogen), and O (Oxygen). To differentiate fats from sugar, fats have nearly twice the number of H as C and a very small number of O. They also form long chains of repetitive molecules.
- **Proteins**: are composed of **amino acids** and are made based on the original DNA sequence. All proteins contain C, H, O and N (Nitrogen). The nitrogen in particular sets them apart, as fats and sugars will rarely if ever contain nitrogen.
- **Nucleic acids** are biomolecules like **DNA and RNA**. Nucleic acids consist of a sugar group, a P (Phosphorus) group and a base containing N in addition to C, H, and O.

...................................................................................................................

### Basic definitions for chemical reactions

- **Reactant**: substances at the beginning of a reaction
- **Products**: substances at the end of a reaction
- **Solute**: substances which dissolve in solvent
- **Solvent**: the liquid in which a solute is dissolved to form a solution
- **Solution**: a homogenous mixture of two or more components

...................................................................................................................

**Kinetic vs. Potential energy: Kinetic energy** is the energy which an object contains because of a particular motion. **Potential energy** is the stored energy, when an object is in a state of rest.

...................................................................................................................

**Classifications of Living Things**: More specifically, knowing that a species is the lowest (or most specific) form of classification and falls within the larger classifications (like genus and family)

...................................................................................................................

**Dominant vs. Recessive Traits:** When genes that code for particular traits combine, they need to decide who comes out on top. For example, you can only have one hair color, so if your mother has brown hair and your father has red hair, one of those two traits is going to manifest itself in you. The one that's more likely to win is called a **dominant trait,** and the one that's more likely to lose is called a **recessive trait.** Using the example above, let's assume brown hair is a dominant trait and red hair is recessive. We represent the "dominance" of a trait by giving it a capital letter, "B" and the recessive is lowercase "r."

The traits can combine in one of four possible ways according to this table:

| BB | rB |
|---|---|
| Br | rr |

In all of the available circumstances where a "B" is present, it will win out over the "r," and you would have brown hair with a 75% probability. However, there is a 25% chance in the 4th case where both genes combine as a recessive pair, "rr," and you would have red hair. So which trait will win is left to chance, but the dominance sets the odds in advance.

# PRACTICE READING THE PASSAGES

The next few pages will contain some sample science passages of varying types. Some will include sample annotations/notes, while others are left blank. For those that are blank, practice reading through the information quickly while searching for (and marking up) the most relevant details. Remember to be on the lookout for:

- Purpose: What is the author trying to achieve with this study? What specific area of science are we dealing with and why is this specific study going to help make a finding?

- Operations: Do not read focus on these details intensely on the first read-through, but make note of where they are. Think about why the scientist took the specific steps that he or she took. What are the functions of the various tools the scientist is using such as measurement devices? Considering this can help with the questions that relate to operations and "why" the scientist did something.

    - Ex: Why did the scientist place a flask in a bed of sand and then put a heat source below? The scientist did this so the heat would distribute more evenly rather than place heat directly on the flask.

- Graphs: Take a look at what information is presented on each graph. What variables are at play? How do the graphs help to differentiate the different studies?

- Variables: Make sure that you know what each variable represents.

- Generalized outcomes: Try to make generalizations about the outcomes. Look for direct and indirect relationships. Don't hyperfocus on specific data points but rather try to synthesize the passage as a whole.

    - Ex: As the amount of fertilizer increased, the size of the tomato fruits increased. When the fertilizer volume reached a certain point the plants were over-fertilized, the tomato plants started to die and therefore the fruit size decreased.

## Formation of the Elements

Scientists are discussing how the elements heavier than iron formed in the galaxy. They base their arguments on the astronomical observations, and they notice that elements such as strontium and barium have abundances in very old stars that are similar to the abundances in our own solar system, which is a very young system. Each scientist makes the following claims.

### Scientist 1

The heavy elements are formed in the neutron star mergers. In these events, two neutron stars collide, and the very neutron-rich matter that is ejected into space undergoes nuclear reaction processes to create the very heavy elements. This process is capable of producing a large amount of heavy elements in significant abundances. For example, neutron star mergers are capable of producing a large amount of barium, an element observed in the solar system and throughout our galaxy in abundance. Stellar explosions cannot possibly produce the heavy elements because they do not produce enough barium to match the abundances observed in our solar system. Other exotic processes, such as magneto-hydrodynamic jets can't be responsible for the production of these elements because they are simply too rare.

### Scientist 2

Heavy elements are formed in the type 2 supernovae. In these events, massive stars at the end of their lives explode and eject matter into space, which undergoes neutron capture reactions which ultimately form the heavy elements we see today. Type 2 supernovae are a likely candidate for heavy element formation because they are quite frequent in the galaxy. Because we observe barium everywhere in the galaxy, we need a process that is more frequent and can occur very early on in galactic history. Neutron star mergers cannot be responsible for the formation of heavy elements because they are too infrequent, and they take too long to produce the heavy elements that we observe in very old stars, which were formed very early in the galaxy. Magneto-hydrodynamic jets also eject too little material into space to produce significant amounts of heavy elements.

### Scientist 3

The elements heavier than iron were produced in magneto-hydrodynamic (MHD) jets, exotic processes in which a massive neutron star or black hole ejects a stream of matter into interstellar clouds. This matter would then collide with the clouds, and the super-heated material would undergo the nuclear reactions necessary to produce the heavy elements we see in space.

The amount of material ejected in MHD jets is enhanced by the fact that they are continuously running; thus the material builds up over time.

jets created elements
matter collides with clouds
continuous → material builds up

mergers created elements
abundant
explosions → don't make enough
jets → too rare

explosions created elements
frequent
mergers too infrequent
jets don't make enough

## Amino Acids

Amino acids are molecules used by nearly every living thing. Because they are asymmetric, there are two forms which are mirror images of each other. The "L" form and the "D" form can be produced synthetically, but only the "L" form is present in all living things. Scientists have multiple theories for this. Some of these are:

### Scientist 1

Amino acids are formed on earth in the "L" form. The interactions of circularly polarized light (CPL) can selectively destroy the "D" form, leaving only the "L" form. Life then evolves using only the "L" form. Amino acids cannot be formed in space because the transport to earth would destroy them upon re-entry into the atmosphere.

### Scientists 2

Amino acids are formed in space in the "L" form via interactions of magnetic and electric fields, which selectively destroy the "D" form. They are then transported to the earth encases in meteorites large enough to survive to the surface. Life then evolves using only the "L" form. CPL cannot be responsible for the formation of the "L" form because it is random in which form it destroys; on average, it would destroy both forms equally.

### Scientist 3

Amino acids are neither selectively destroyed or created; they cannot be produced in a specific form regardless of where they are formed. The "L" form came about to be dominant as life evolved first to use both forms and eventually evolved to use only the "L" form. CPL or magnetic fields cannot form amino acids in a form because they don't produce enough of one particular form to be significant.

**Fish Heart Conditions by Temperature**

Environmental temperature can play a significant role in shaping the size, structure, and function of an animal's organs. Specifically, temperature can change the electrical activity within and around individual cells, determining each cell's *membrane potential*, which is the difference in electric current that carries molecules from one side of a cell membrane to the other. Such changes can limit a cell's ability to transport the specific number of molecular ions required for normal cell function.

*temp affects cell function*

Fish are distinct from mammals in that the temperature of their body is regulated by the temperature of their environment. Therefore, fish have developed multiple physical adaptations to help them cope with changing temperatures. Scientists have determined that fish hearts contract highly under cold conditions, impacting the flow of ions and ability of their heart muscles to contract and pump blood.

*fish adapt*

Figure 1 illustrates the changes in calcium ion flow, △F, measured in pA units of electrical current, across varying membrane potentials, MP, (in millivolts) in water at different temperatures

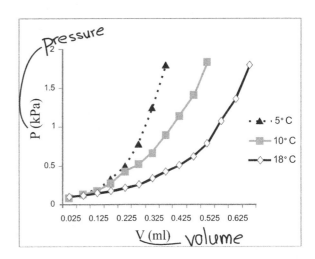

Figure 3 shows changes in amounts of compact and spongy tissue in fish ventricles under different temperatures.

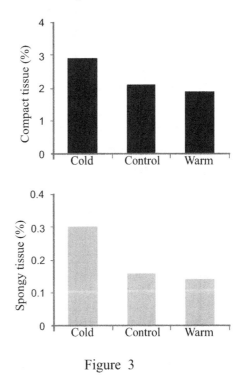

Figure 3

Figures and data adopted from Keen AN, Klaiman JM, Shiels HA, and Gillis TE (2017) Temperature-induced cardiac remodelling in fish. Journal of Experimental Biology 220, 147-160 doi:10.1242/jeb.128496.

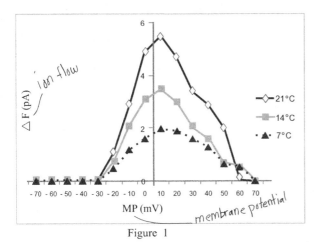

Figure 1

Figure 2 shows changes in the pressure, P, and volume, V, of *ventricles* (blood-pumping chambers) in a fish heart under different temperatures.

## Mixtures

When two substances mix, three possible mixtures may form. They are called solutions, colloids, and suspensions. The mixtures may form from substances in either the solid, liquid, or gas phase. The mixtures are classified based on the physical characteristics expressed.

Table 1 lists the type of mixture and some of their general characteristics as well as approximates the particle size of the substance mixed in water. 1 nanometer (nm) = $10^{-9}$ meters (m).

| Table 1 | | | |
|---|---|---|---|
| **Mixture characteristic** | **Aquous solution** | **Aqueous colloid** | **Aqueus suspension** |
| **Approximate particle diameter (nm)\*** | <1m | 1-1,00 nm | >1,000 nm |
| **Clarity under intense light** | Clear | Cloudy | Opaque |
| **Interaction with light** | Light shines through | Light is scattered | Light cannot shine through |
| **Particle settling** | Particles do not settle | Particle do not settle | Particle settle after sometime |
| **Particle filterability** | Particle do not filter | Particle do not filter | Particle time |
| **Particle visibility** | Cannot see | Can only see with microscope | Can see with naked eyes |
| \* These approximate particle sizes also applies to non-aqueous mixtures. | | | |

Table 2 lists some common colloids made from substances in various phases. In a mixture, the major component is called the *dispersion medium* while the minor component is called the *dispersed material*.

| Table 2 | | | |
|---|---|---|---|
| **Dipersion medium** | **Dispersed material** | | |
| | **Gas** | **Liquid** | **Solid** |
| **Gas** | None | Aerosol (fog) | Aerosol (smoke) |
| **Liquid** | Foam (shaving cream) | Emulsion (milk) | Sol (paint) |
| **Solid** | Solid foam (Styrofoam) | Solid emulsion (butter) | Solid sol (steel) |

## Study of Solvents

Scientists interested in studying the effects of three different solvents on the rate of dissolving conducted three experiments. The results are shown below.

### Experiment 1

Scientists took a tablet of a common antacid and placed it in a 100-ml beaker A. They took another tablet and cut it in half and placed both halves in 100 ml beaker B. They then proceeded to take additional tablets and cut them into smaller sections and placed them into additionally labeled 100-ml beakers. 5 0 ml of water at 1°C was added to each beaker and the time the tablet took to completely dissolve, D, was measured in seconds.

| Table 1 | | |
|---|---|---|
| Beaker | Tablet piece size | D (s) |
| A | Whole | 181 |
| B | 1/2 | 92 |
| C | 1/4 | 47 |
| D | 1/8 | 23 |
| E | 1/16 | 11 |
| F | 1/32 | 5 |

### Experiment 2

Scientists placed a whole tablet of antacid in each of 100 ml beakers labeled A-F. Each beaker received 50 ml of water at various temperatures, T. The time the table took to completely dissolve, D, was recorded in seconds.

| Table 2 | | |
|---|---|---|
| Beaker | T (°C) | D (s) |
| A | 1 | 190 |
| B | 15 | 144 |
| C | 30 | 101 |
| D | 45 | 70 |
| E | 60 | 49 |
| F | 75 | 38 |

### Experiment 3

Scientists placed a whole tablet of antacid in each of 100-ml beakers labeled A–F. Each beaker received 50 ml of various solvents at a temperature of 1°C. The time the tablet took to completely dissolve, D was recorded in seconds.

| Table 3 | | |
|---|---|---|
| Beaker | D (s) | Solvent |
| A | 185 | Water |
| B | 167 | Methanol |
| C | 155 | Ethanol |
| D | 34 | Acetic acid (1M) |
| E | 15 | Hydrochloric acid (1M) |
| F | 240 | Hexane |

# SUMMARY

- The science section can be thought of as reading comprehension with the addition of graphs and figures.

- You don't have to read the passages in order. Prioritize the passages you think are easier.

- Prioritize the "easier" questions, especially if you're short on time.

- Do not spend too much time reading through the passages. Skim for what's important.

- The visuals are arguably the most important part of a passage.

- Simplify the question by rephrasing it in your own words and breaking the ideas apart.

- Annotate the questions and the figures at the same time.

- Arrive at the correct answer by picking the one that pairs with an important element of the experiment.

- Never underestimate the power of giving yourself better odds through the process of elimination!

- Pay close attention to the axes to ensure you are using the correct variables.

- Be mindful of a question's setup

- Refamiliarize yourself with the "science basics."

# FINAL TIPS

## THE NIGHT BEFORE THE EXAM

As crazy as it may sound, this is not the time for studying! Some brief reviewing of your strategy and formula sheets can be helpful, but you shouldn't be trying to learn any new information or cram in a lot of last-minute practice. Trust that you have done all you can do. Be confident in what you know; don't worry about the things that you don't. Most of all, try to relax. That's easier said than done, we know. But these exams are just as much a mental game as they are anything else, so it's important that you keep your cool and trust in your instincts!

Here are some things you can do the night before your official exam:

- Read through strategy sheets one last time.
- Briefly read through math formula sheet and punctuation sheet.
- Make sure you are prepared for exam day.
    - Gather materials. Make sure you have:
        - Number 2 pencils
        - A calculator (charged and with an extra set of batteries)
        - Your ID and admissions ticket
        - A watch (nothing digital)
        - Water and a snack
    - Have an outfit ready. Dress in layers: you never know how hot or cold your room may be!
    - Make sure you know what location you're going to and how to get there
- Set an alarm
- Set another alarm
- Relax! Don't cram. Do something enjoyable to calm your nerves.
- Get a good night's sleep

## THE MORNING OF THE EXAM

- Eat a good breakfast.
- Work through one or two practice problems that you **know how to do** to get your mind working.
- Make sure you have everything you need.
- Stay calm!

## RESULTS

You can expect your results within two weeks, **typically 10 days after the exam date**. The one major exception is the October exam, which can take 3–8 weeks for scores to be released. The February exam also takes a bit longer (roughly 2 and half weeks).

If you take the optional essay, you can expect to see the essay score about two weeks after your multiple choice scores are released.

If you have testing accommodations, you may need to wait longer for your results. There is no designated release date for exams with accommodations, so just hang tight! You may have to wait a few extra weeks, but some students receive their scores just around the time of the standard release date.

At least twice a year, the ACT will give students the option to purchase a **TIR (Test Information Release) report**. Students will receive a blank copy of the exam and a print-out of their answers. This is an incredibly helpful study tool when preparing for future exams. You can expect this a few weeks after your scores are released. Check the ACT's website for up-to-date information on which exams they are offering this service with and how to register. Typically you will have up to 5 days after the exam to register for the report online.

# 1-TO-1 HELP FROM CURVEBREAKERS
# Virtual Tutoring

SAT ∘ ACT ∘ SSAT ∘ SHSAT ∘ AP EXAMS ∘ REGENTS
SUBJECT TUTORING ∘ STUDY SKILLS

No matter where you live, connect with a tutor in seconds, and enjoy the flexibility of one-on-one tutoring anywhere with an internet connection.

Curvebreakers is a results-focused company that has a proven track record of success. All of our tutoring plans are customized to the individual student's needs based on our incredibly detailed diagnostic system.

First, we virtually administer a fully timed, previously administered exam to find out your starting point. Our detailed score analysis breaks down the results to make sure each students knows exactly where she needs to focus.

Curvebreakers will formulate a plan based on data and YOU. Through our virtual classroom, we will work with you to take the appropriate and most effective steps you need to improve your score.

Don't waste time with tutors who don't fully understand these exams. Curvebreakers' tutors are required to have scored in the 99th-percentile on the SAT or ACT and are trained in the same flexible and adaptable methodology.

- See How it Works
- Find our package rates
- Contact us with questions
- Watch a Video to learn more!

Made in the USA
Coppell, TX
02 November 2020